Desire and Dust

Roee Rosen

Sternberg Press

This book is created as part of the exhibition
Roee Rosen: The Mosquito-Mouse and Other Hybrids
at Kunsthal Charlottenborg.

Desire and Dust
Roee Rosen

Featuring:
The Dust Files by Paul B. Preciado
The Biography of the Object by Sergei Tret́iakov

Kunsthal Charlottenborg
Billedkunstskolernes Forlag
Sternberg Press

Contents

The Potential of Hybrids
(Thoughts, Content and Thanks)

Foreword by Anne Mikél Jensen

Can fiction be more real than reality? Can hybrids teach us about politics? How do we remember the past, and is satire a tool for both subalterns and power players? These are just some of the thoughts that went through my mind while working on the exhibition *The Mosquito-Mouse and Other Hybrids* by visual artist, writer and director Roee Rosen. This pocketbook now expands the exhibition with six compelling texts relating to the above, including a new commission by Paul B. Preciado, which literally brings Roee Rosen's work to new places.

We have compiled poems, historical jokes, a sci-fi text based on files from Mars, a retro-garde manifesto and biographies of both objects and subjects. Together with images of artworks, stills and sketches they visualize works from *The Mosquito-Mouse and Other Hybrids* as well as the process behind them.

The first text, *Vengeful Animism*, is Rosen's biographical introduction to his fictive persona Maxim Komar-Myshkin, who is the leading persona behind all the works in the exhibition as well as the supposed author of most other texts in this book. Komar-Myshkin's magnum opus and the centerpiece of the exhibition is the gouache series *Vladimir's Night*, in which animated objects do violence to the protagonist, Vladimir.[1] In the present volume, *Desire and Dust*, you can find earlier literary exercises by Komar-Myshkin in which he magically endows still objects with life. Two of the three poems tell a specific commodity its own corporate life story and qualities, while the third poem attempts to bring life to a hybrid of objects through neologisms reminiscent of Russian Avant-Garde poets. One of these awakening poems for commodities became the libretto of Rosen's major cinematographic work, *The Dust Channel*, which tells the story of a bourgeois couple whose fear of dirt, dust and any foreign matter results in a ménage à trois between them and their Dyson DC07, a vacuum cleaner which not only is an object of desire but also has a will of its own. The playful, perverse and private obsessions conveyed here enter the somber realm of another fear and other invasions by exposing the xenophobic policy meted against refugees.

The Dust Channel is the raison d'être for Paul B. Preciado's *The Dust Files*, a sci-fi text with facts from space about techno-sexuality, socio-political phobias, kinship, and the understanding of belonging. *The Dust Files* is followed by a manifesto, authored by Maxim Komar-Myshkin's fictive collective, the Buried Alive group, after which you can read historical jokes written by Maxim Komar-Myshkin himself. These jokes originate from a literary work Komar-Myshkin was unable to complete: an entire history of Russia made of jokes. Lastly, you will find a classic from 1929: *The Biography of the Object* by the Russian constructivist critic Sergei Tret́iakov. Tret́iakov's polemical argument, that we should focus on telling the tales of things rather than of privileged individuals so as to bring forth the assembly lines and class relations, can be key to the understanding of Komar-Myshkin's twisted object biographies, as well as to Preciado's futuristic spin on Rosen's *Dust Channel*. The two authors manage, like Tret́iakov, to unlearn the prevailing while unpacking new realities through fiction. Altogether, this publication aims to be a pocketbook about dissolving borders, the understanding of desire, belonging, fear, the instrumentalization of historical traumas and cultural legacy. Bring it with you on the road and let it guide or inspire you – no matter what solar system you inhabit.

Kunsthal Charlotttenborg would sincerely like to thank the Grosserer L. F. Foght's Foundation, the Knud Højgaard's Foundation, the Obel Family Foundation and the Danish Arts Foundation for financial support. Also, thanks for the support, help and contributions to colleagues and friends of the house, Rosenfeld Gallery, Orna Agmon, Paul B. Preciado, *October*/MIT, James Copeland and Laura Preston. Above all we would like to thank the wonderful and clever Roee Rosen, whom it has been inspirational and exciting to work with.

1 *Vladimir's Night* has been published as a separate book, in which annotations of its text and images become a veritable novel: Roee Rosen, Maxim Komar-Myshkin, *Vladimir's Night* (Sternberg Press, 2014).

Vengeful Animism:
On Maxim Komar-Myshkin's "Vladimir's Night"

by Roee Rosen

Vladimir's Night is a hybrid of a children book, an exceedingly gory martyrdom and, perhaps, a twisted political treatise. Here, Vladimir (Putin, although the name is never mentioned) is both a little child and a political leader vacationing in his summer mansion. Before falling asleep, he imagines seeing faces in the wooden veneer of his bedroom cabinet. The faces move, a mouth opens up, and out of the closet flow animated mundane objects, soon to be joined by over-lively friends hailing from Vladimir's drawer, his bag and from the outside. What begins as merry frolicking between boy and objects soon turns violent: Vladimir is molested, tortured and finally murdered by them.

The fictive Russian author and artist Efim Poplavsky (1978–2011) always maintained that he was neither an artist nor an author. His pseudonym, Maxim Komar-Myshkin, connotes in Russian a mouse and a mosquito, and he perceived his work through the attributes of these animals: the mosquito, parasitically feeding on the blood of "big" and "real" humans (be they powerful politicians or venerated cultural personae), and the mouse, feasting on leftovers and stashed goods and connoting infiltration and dirt. Both mouse and mosquito suggest a nuisance rather than a major threat (yet, given the right circumstances, they can become deadly), and both are domestically present even as they strive to remain hidden and invisible. Poplavsky thus described whatever he was discreetly producing as "private dreck."

While "Myshkin" obviously nods to Dostoevsky's protagonist in *The Idiot*, Poplavsky's *nom de plume* is a triple homage to the Russian writer Daniil Kharms. "Maxim" is a Russian name, but it happens to have a Hebrew meaning: "charming" (and Kharms reputedly chose his own pen name to echo the English words "charms" and "harms"); Myshkin is the name of the protagonist of one of Kharms very short stories, and "Komar" is derived from "Komarov," a character in another. Komar-Myshkin was deeply influenced by Kharms' funny and horrifying sense of the absurd, epitomizing for him two seemingly incommensurate states: an exhilarating, defiant and irrational autonomy through art, and an all-encompassing sense of realistic terror and doom from an author who suffered persecution in Stalin's USSR and perished in a prison hospital in 1942.

Soon after Komar-Myshkin immigrated to Israel in the late '90s, he founded the Buried Alive group, a tightly knit collective of ex-Soviet young artists, actors, musicians and writers. Here again the name is telling, for it conveys not only the rather morbid sense of humor typical of the group but the schizophrenic spirit of its activities. Buried Alive were resolutely alienated from the local Israeli cultural scene towards which they felt inherently superior, yet they were also experiencing the tremendous hardship and insecurity stemming from their seclusion. For Buried Alive, the Moscow unofficial artists of the '60s and the '70s were thus not only a main source of artistic influence (*Vladimir's Night* is akin in form to the earlier albums produced by artists such as Ilya Kabakov and Viktor Pivovarov); they saw themselves as continuing the autonomous, intimate and publicly unrecognized existence that typified the Moscow circle: a self-sustaining artistic scene devoid of hierarchies or material value, based entirely on personal friendships and passionate commitment. For Poplavsky, however, the name also conveyed the actual fear explored in Edgar Allan Poe's tale *The Premature Burial*, colored by the acute paranoia he suffered from.

It was only two years before he committed suicide that I met Poplavsky. At the time, I was working on a film about the Israeli minister of foreign affairs, Avigdor Lieberman, and needed help researching Russian texts and interviews. I was struck from the start by the contrast between Poplavsky's sober irony, and his fits of conspiratorial suspicion and anxiety, which, I was all too soon to learn, indicated greater suffering than I imagined. For Efim Poplavsky believed that Putin had a personal vendetta against him, and that even though he was anonymous, unemployed, and had left Russia more than a decade ago, he believed he was a pertinent target for assassination attempts. In fact, for a long span I was certain this fear was a long-winding joke, and once I realize it was not, I could not eke from him any details as to the reasons or the signs for this threat – although I know these were ubiquitous and clear to him. *Vladimir's Night*, in that sense, was Poplavsky's secretive artistic retaliation: animism literally employed to avenge a nemesis.

Poplavsky's notion of animism was highly indebted to Freud, but, much like Breton and Dalí, he was interested neither in the progressive speculations Freud employed (relegating animism to the arcane and the primitive), nor in the therapeutic horizon and scientific claims of psychoanalysis. Rather, he was enthralled by the radical potentials he saw Freud as releasing in regard to the power of the uncanny, and of animism to destabilize the very form (he would say "the body") of art. In this sense, the unlikely hybrid presented in *Vladimir's Night* was for him conveying that existence as being more than one, disavowing the border between the imaginary and the real, never classifiable, always disorienting, in other words: truthful. We can perhaps glimpse that experience of reality through one image in the book: that of the soul that leaps out of Putin's body not in its traditional incarnation as a butterfly, but rather as a mouse-mosquito chimera. It will be recalled that Freud mentions the soul when he discusses the trope of the *doppelgänger*. Like many uncanny motifs, Freud suggests, the double is the monstrous return of something that was once consoling: the soul as a perfect double, immune to physical agony and, ultimately, immune to death. That the soul would turn into a blood-sucking mongrel is thus not only euphoric and horrific; it also posits the author himself as rising from within Putin's body, presenting an aporia by which we cannot tell whether the artist is an alien exterminating its host, or whether, in some way, Vladimir was Maxim all along, identification was ludicrously at play, and the act of revenge was also suicidal.

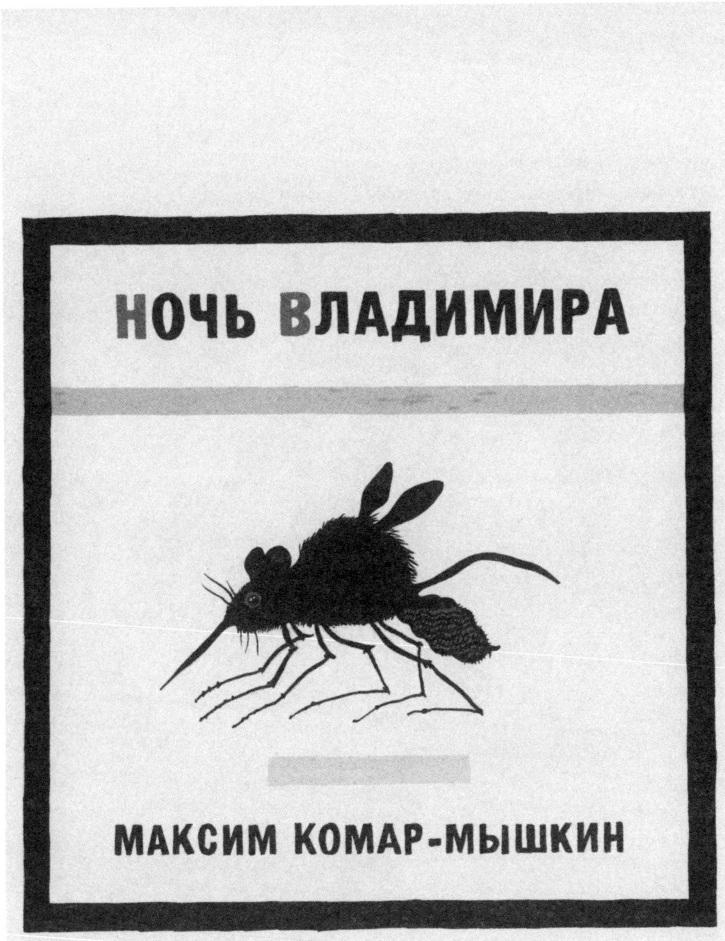

Part of the exhibition *Roee Rosen: The Mosquito-Mouse and Other Hybrids*, 2019

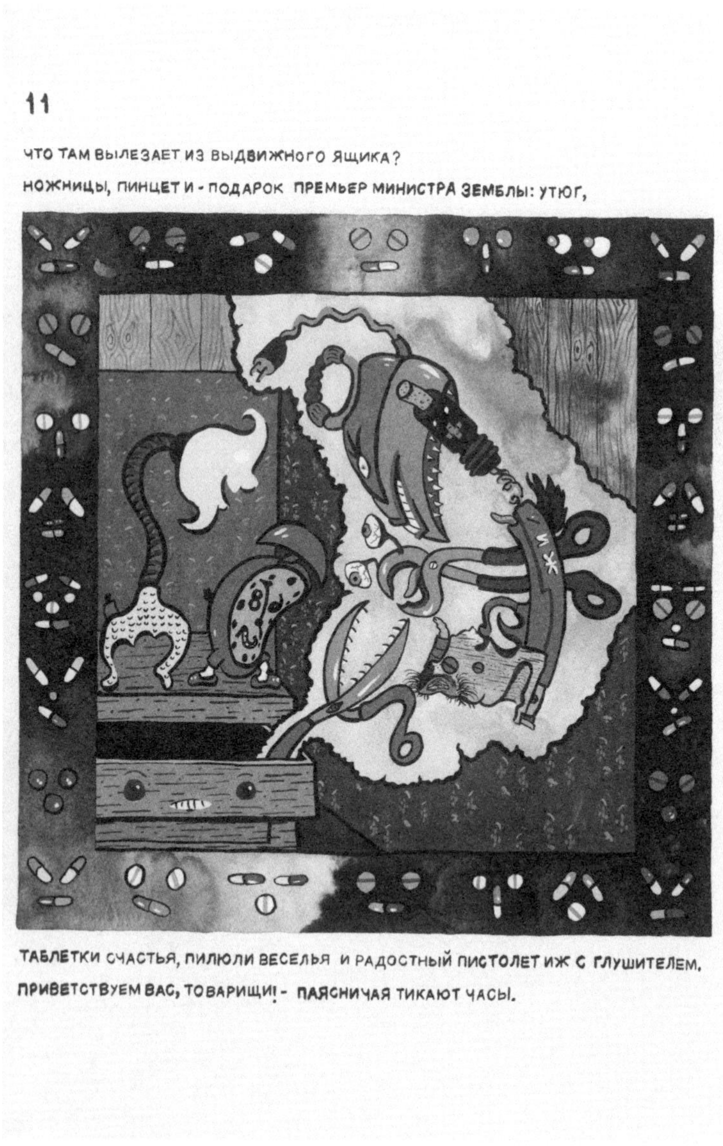

Part of the exhibition *Roee Rosen: The Mosquito-Mouse and Other Hybrids*, 2019

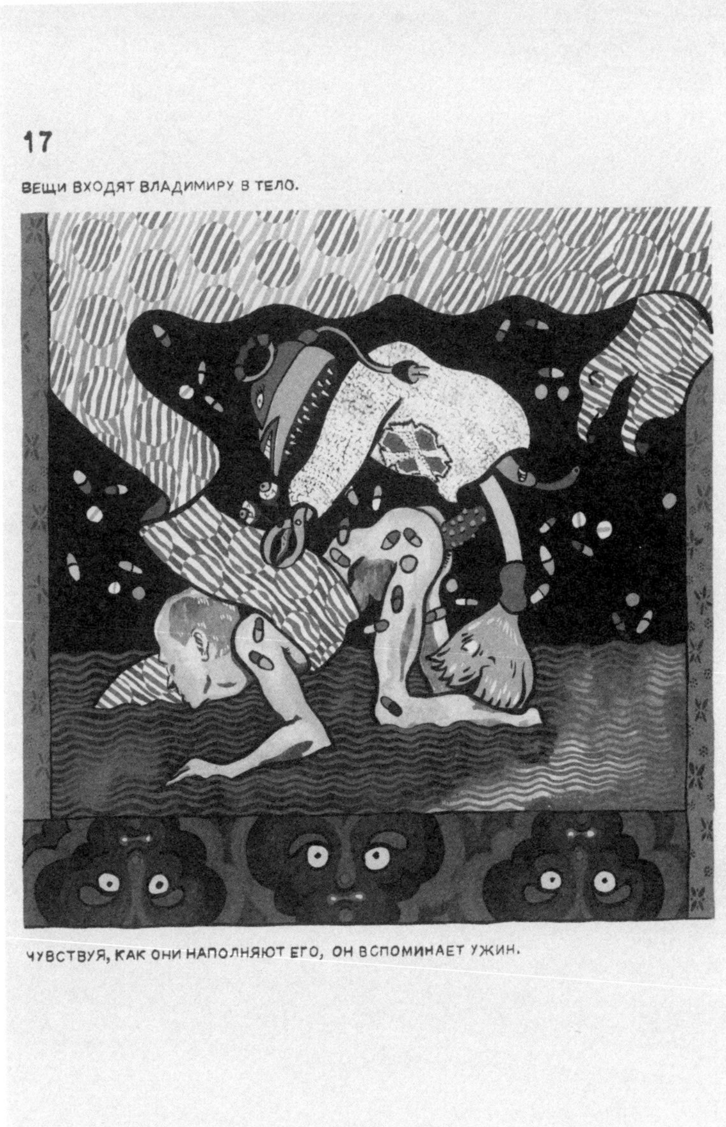

Part of the exhibition *Roee Rosen: The Mosquito-Mouse and Other Hybrids*, 2019

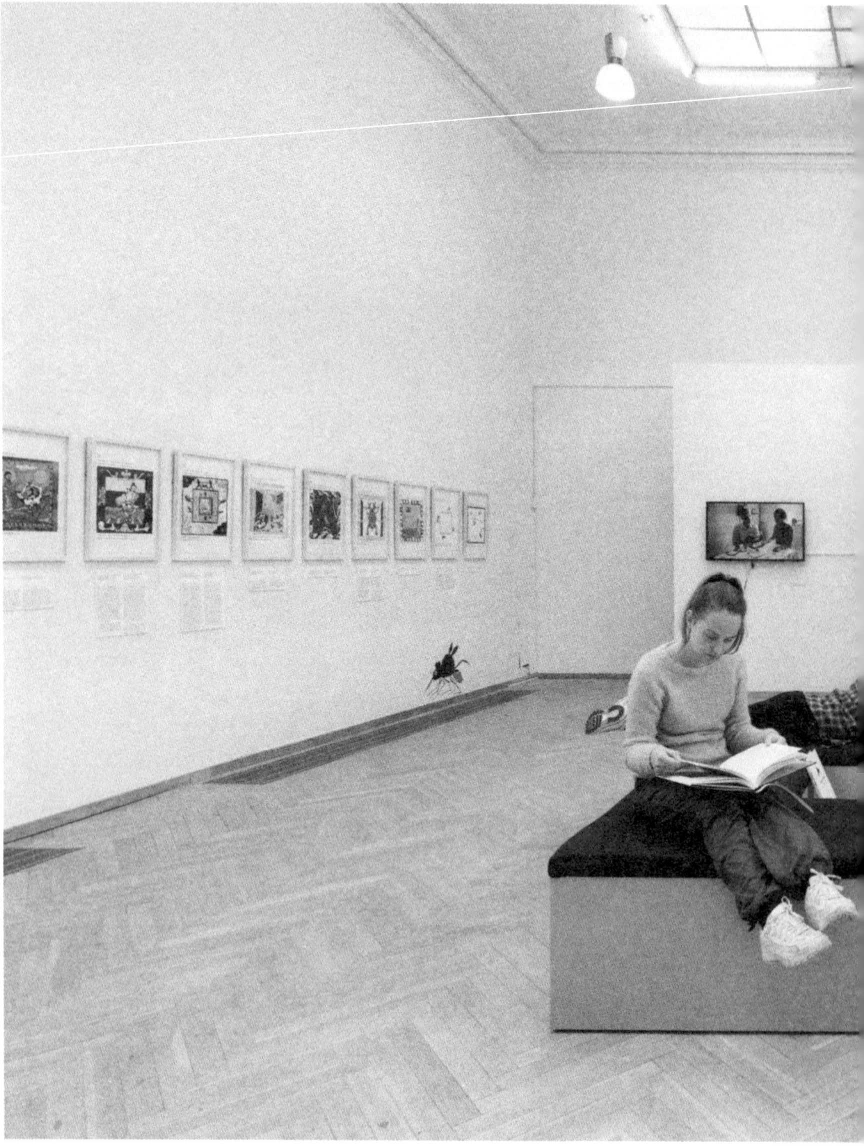

Roee Rosen: The Mosquito-Mouse and Other Hybrids, 2019

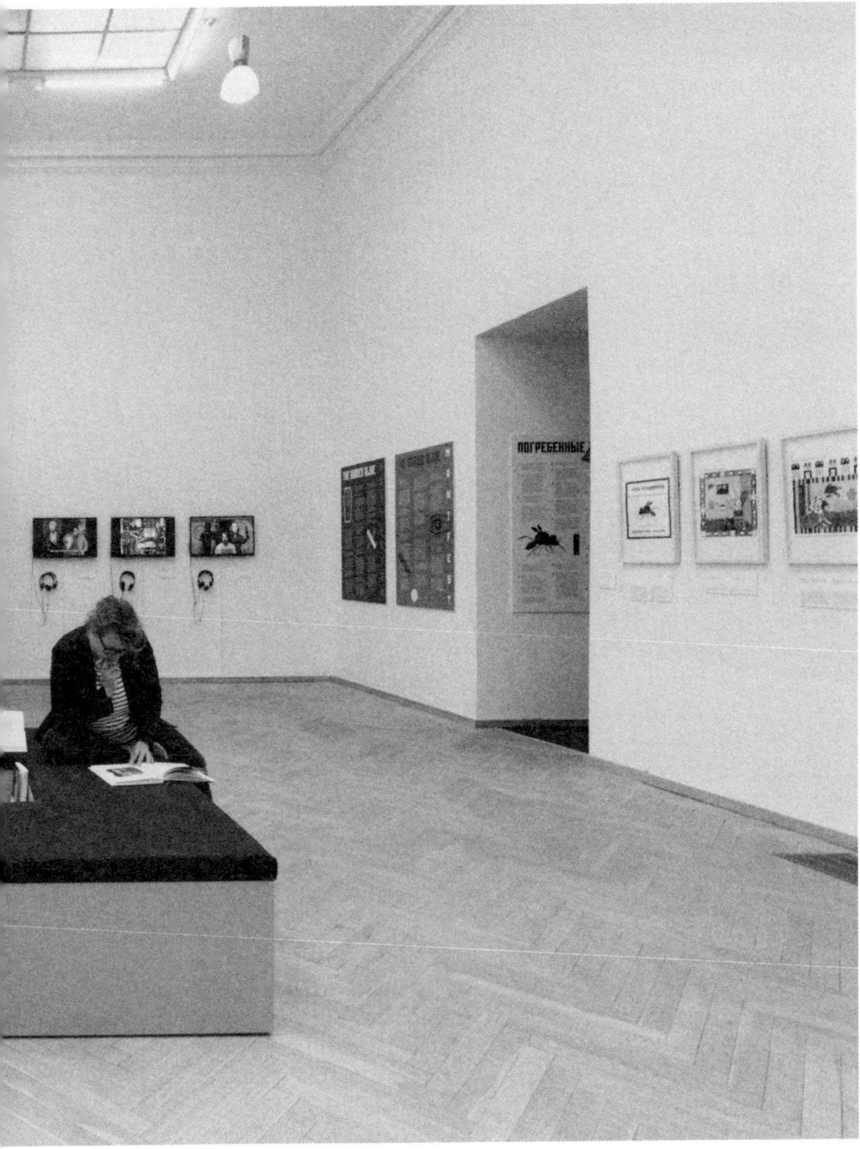
ПОГРЕБЕННЫЕ

Animation Chants for Commodities (1–3)

Little Iron

DC07 Vacuum Cleaner

Hybrid

by Maxim Komar-Myshkin

Animation Chants for Commodities (1)
Little Iron

Wake up, little iron,
Live and love, little iron,
Move about, little iron,
Please try, little iron.

You come from England, Morphy Richrads is your brand
Misters Morphy and Richards opened factory in 1936.
By '38, 400 irons were produced a day and it was grand.
Soon they added other home appliances to the mix.

You're safely grasped by your heat-resistant corky handle.
Everyone knows how hot and mighty your bottom quickly turns.
They use you for domestic help, but there's a fear of you they hardly handle,
knowing you can bring disaster, fire, awful torture, nasty burns.

Wake up, little iron,
Live and love, little iron,
Move about, little iron,
Please try, little iron.

In 1960 Morphy sold his shares to EMI,
And after many wars your company was won by Glen Dimplex,
A privately owned mogul of electric goods, one fateful day in May.
And all that time you seem so modest, yet none can guess your secrets or your sex!

Your wire is your handsome tail, finely dotted white on black,
But it is also your leash, an umbilical chord, tying you to the wall and to your energy supply.
Your metallic nose is pointed and can be a mighty weapon, able skulls to crack;
May it soon succeed to to smell, to smile, and lead you forward, upwards, to the sky!

Wake up, little iron,
Live and love, little iron,
Move about, little iron,
Please try, little iron.

Animation Chants for Commodities (2)

DC07 Vacuum Cleaner [The Libretto for the Cinematic Operetta *The Dust Channel*]

Up, Dyson Seven, Up, Up, Up!
Rise, Dyson Seven, Up, Up, Up!
Breathe, Dyson Seven, Deep, Deep, Deep!
In, Dyson Seven, Suck, Suck, Suck!

Who can recount your many merits, or your splendid history?
They say sir James tried 5,000 prototypes for his first machine.
That's how great Sir James is, and that's how great your beauty and your glory:
Michelangelo did not draw as many sketches for his Sistine!

Hoover's cleaners clogged; Sir James devised solutions, for he's kin and able.
The giant brands aimed to deny him, for dirty is the field of cleaning.
He sold Japan the G-force cleaner, which magically folds into a table;
'Twas a thing of beauty and desire all Asians found appealing.

Up, Dyson Seven, Up, Up, Up!
Rise, Dyson Seven, Up, Up, Up!
Breathe, Dyson Seven, Deep, Deep, Deep!
In, Dyson Seven, Suck, Suck, Suck!

Scum is on display through your transparent belly, as if it were the Grimy Channel.
Thus with you, the abject is pretty to behold, the dust becomes pristine.
Sacred Seven marks your generation and your special seven funnels,
As they perform their cleaning duty, more glorious than Michelangelo's Sistine!

Recently, Sir James declared that foreign students steal knowledge and in secrecy
Plant harmful bugs in our racially pure computers; pray tell if he's a bigot basket-
Case, or if those cunning Asians really do concoct conspiracies.
We're all like carpets, craving suction action – for dirty, dirty is the cleaning market!

Up, Dyson Seven, Up, Up, Up!
Rise, Dyson Seven, Up, Up, Up!
Breathe, Dyson Seven, Deep, Deep, Deep!
In, Dyson Seven, Suck, Suck, Suck!

Animation Chants for Commodities (3)
A Hybrid

Trousers, Rake, Pitchfork, Beads!
Yeast, Scissors, Tweezers!
Lotion, Shavings, Pliers!
Macaroni, Money, Boots!
Trousers, Rake, Pitchfork, Beads!
Uzi, Panties and a Watch! Oh!

Treaded Trousers taste TearTofu,
Yiestor-Tweezor Shiver Freezers,
Lick-a-Lotion Cunniliquorish,
Trousers, Rake, Pitchfork, Beads!
Come to Life!
Come to Life!

Sketches, *Vladimir's Night*, 2011–14

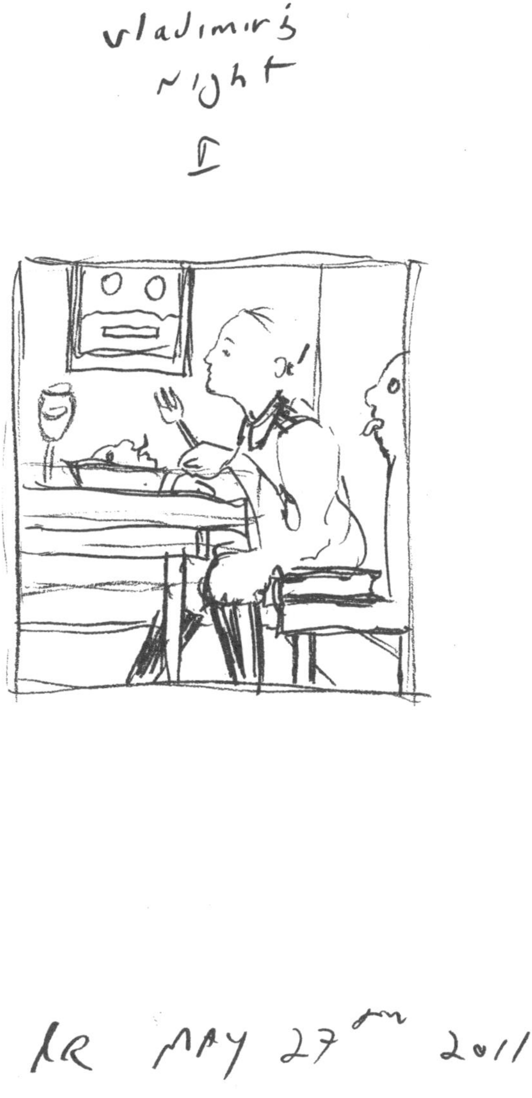

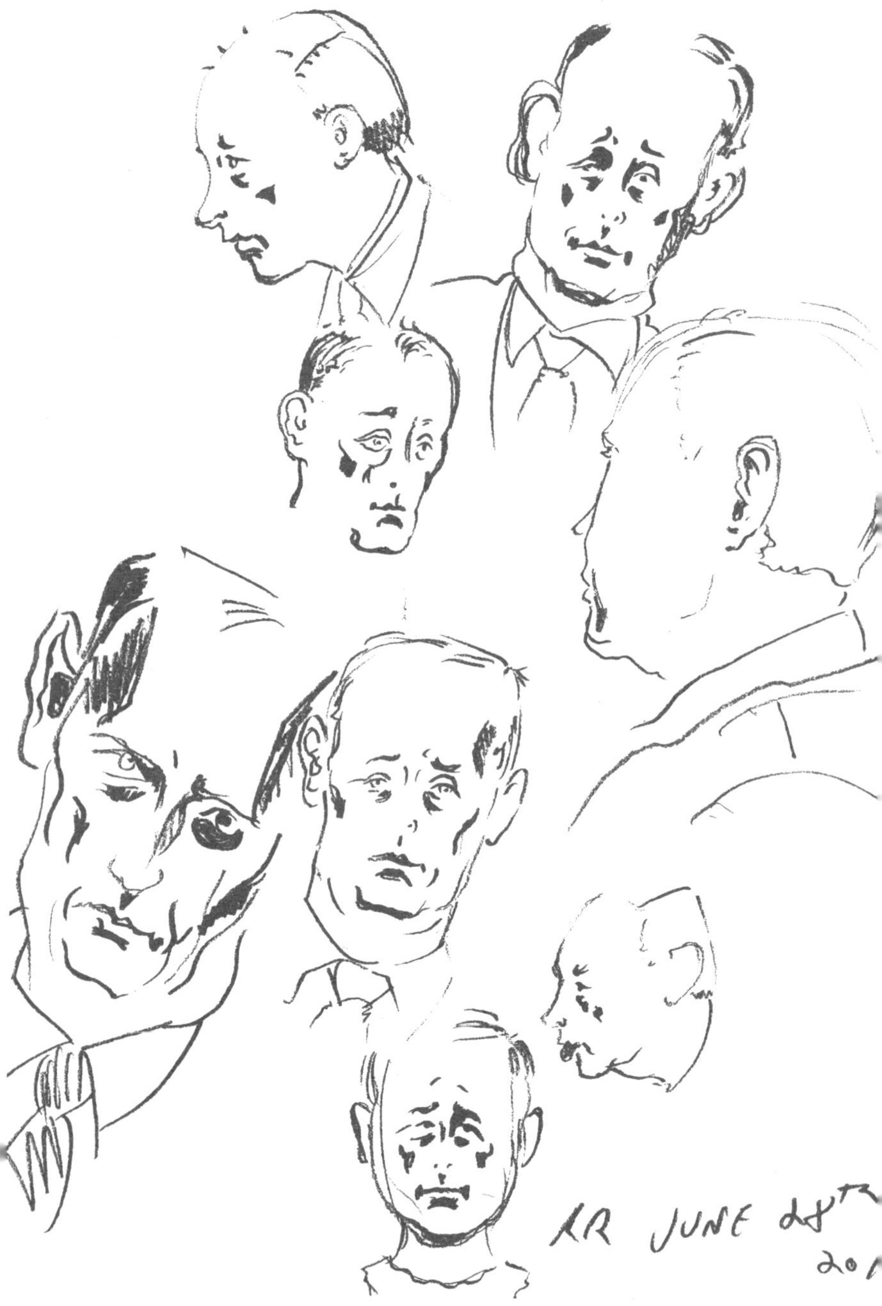
KR JUNE 28TH
201

yellow
Green
Green
ЮКОС

ld JUL 23 2011

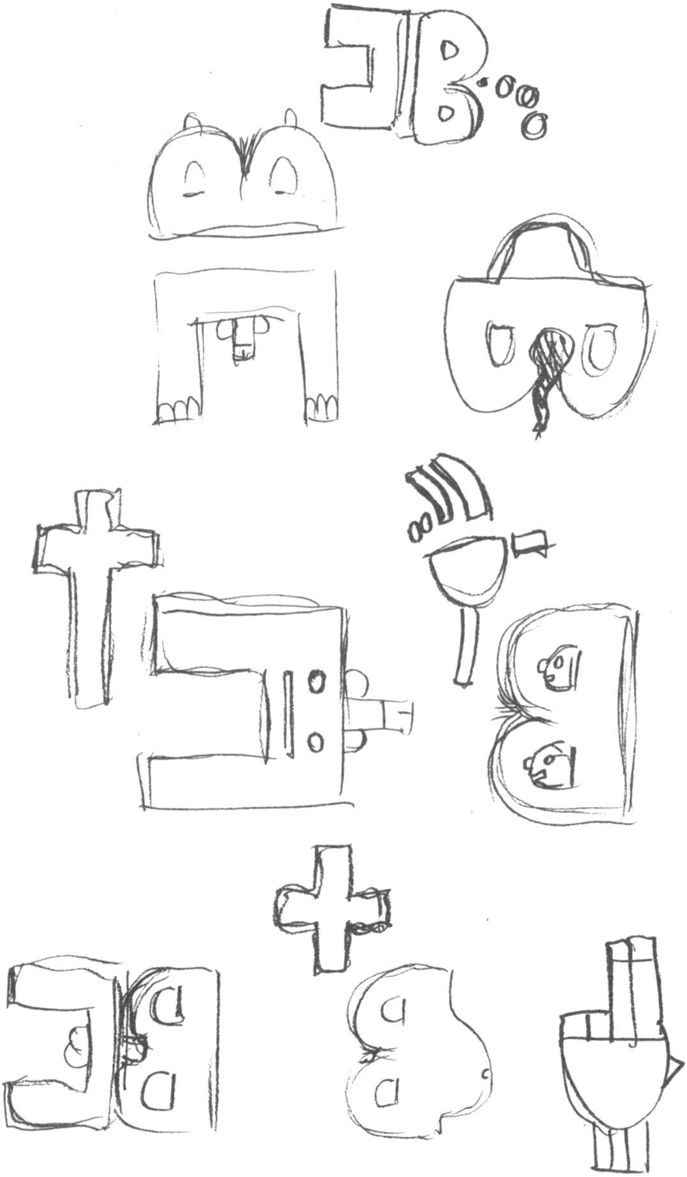

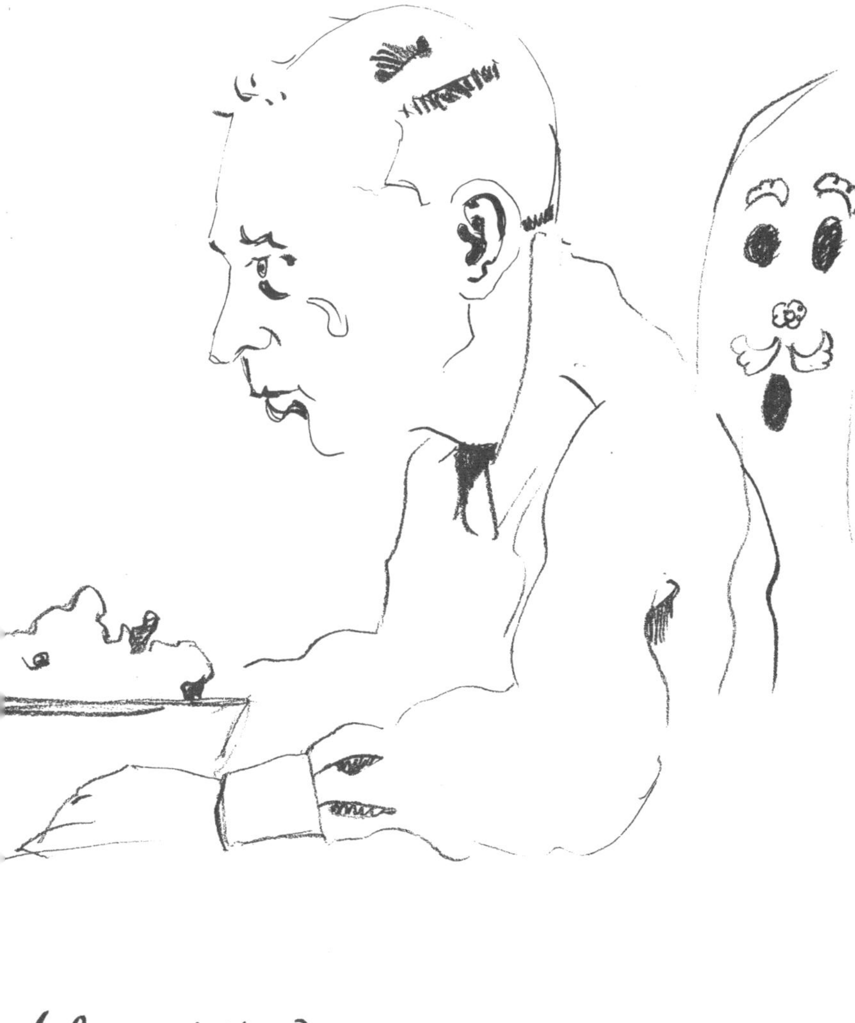

AR, JUL 2 2011

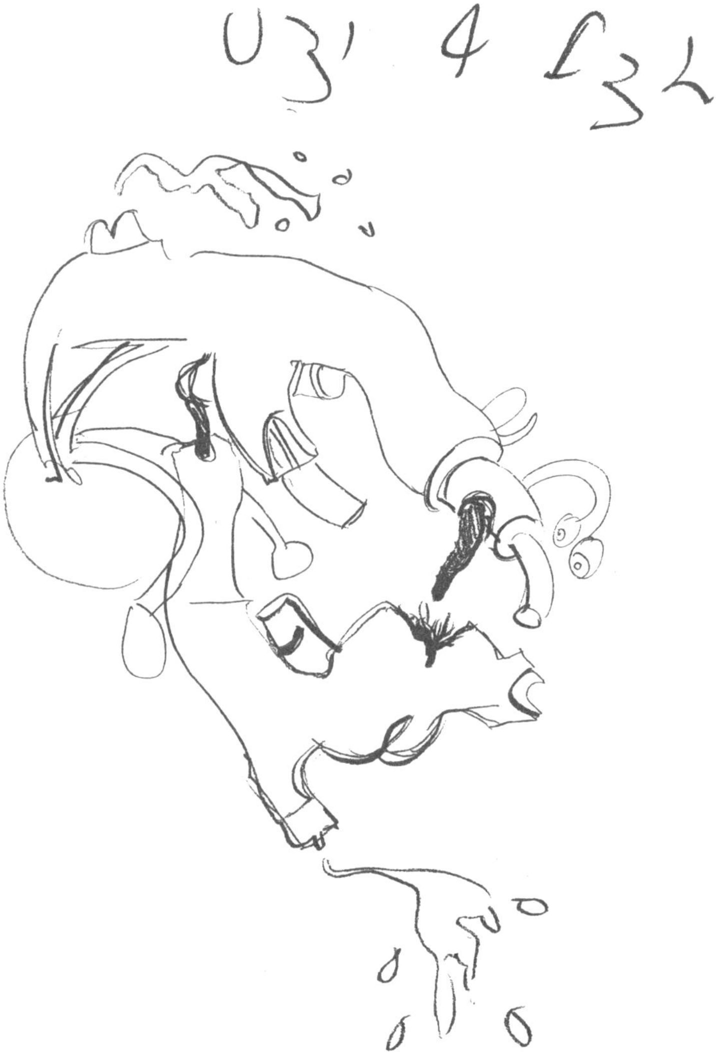

RR AUG 14 2011

face & "helmet" & "Arms" – 1939
+
bottom – 1954

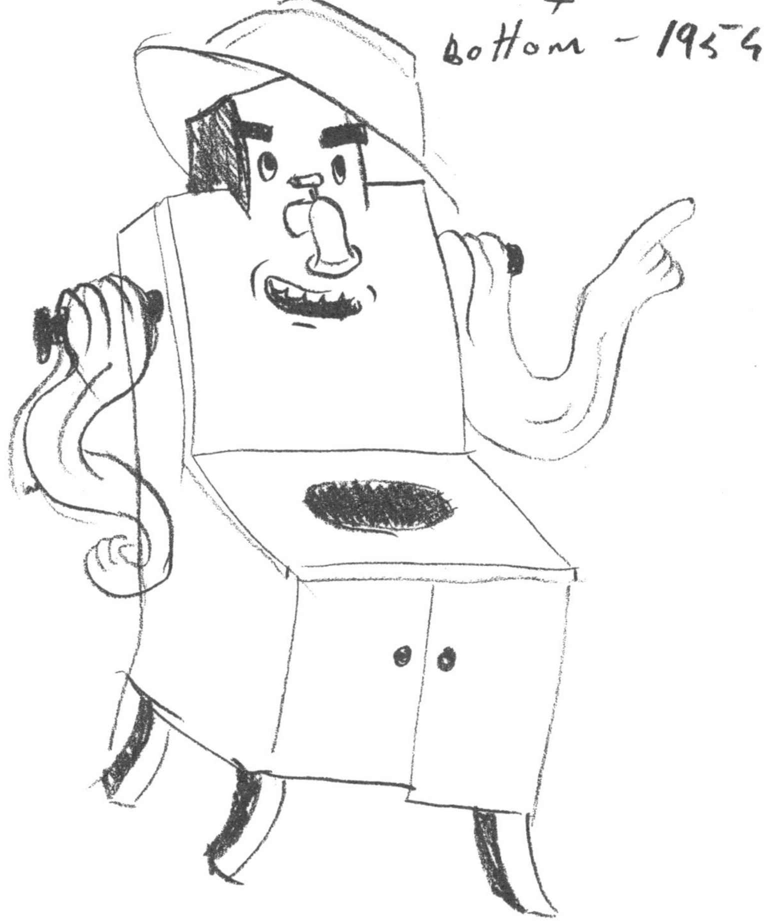

мойдодыр

RR Aug 27 2011

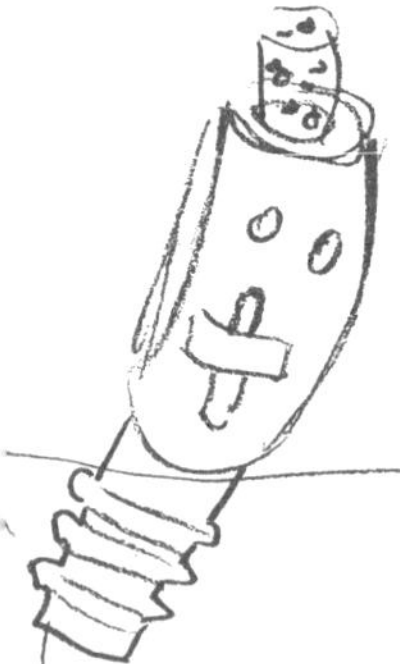

scissors (15), iron (13) 11
pincers, 13h (silencer)
pills + caplets

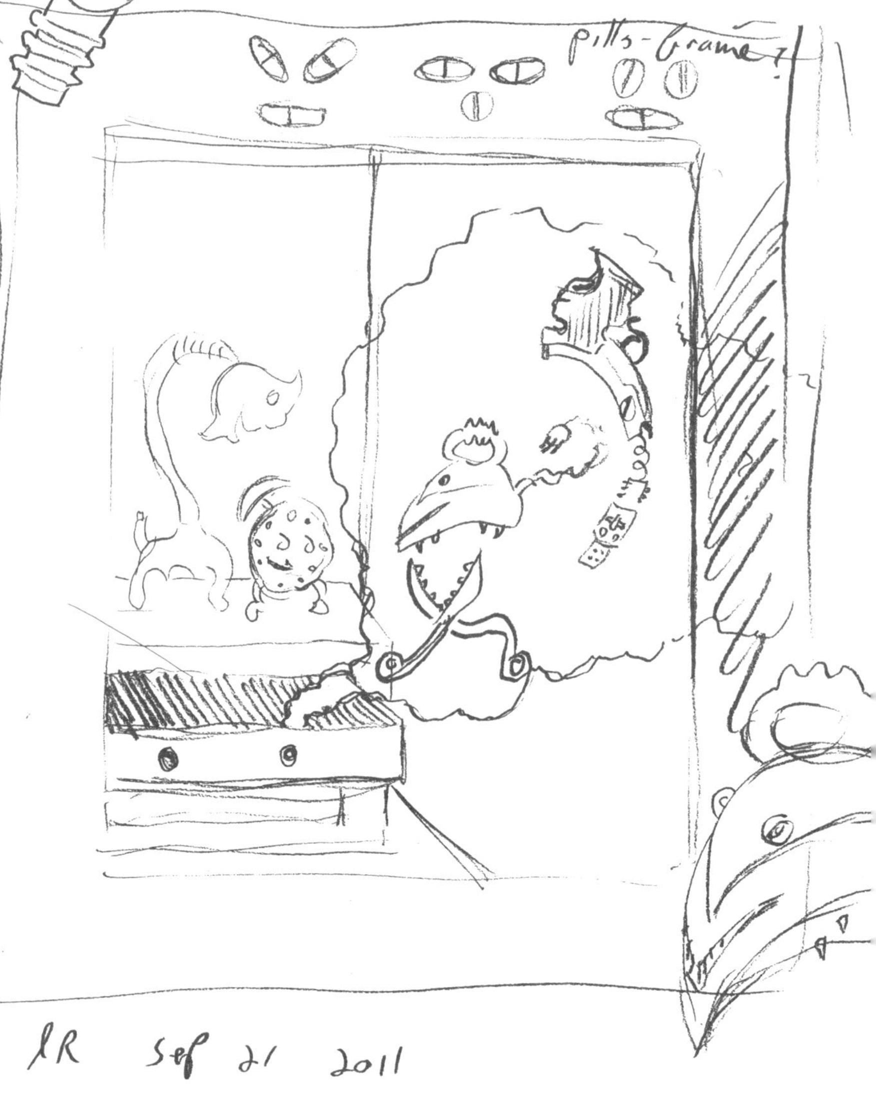

LR Sep 21 2011

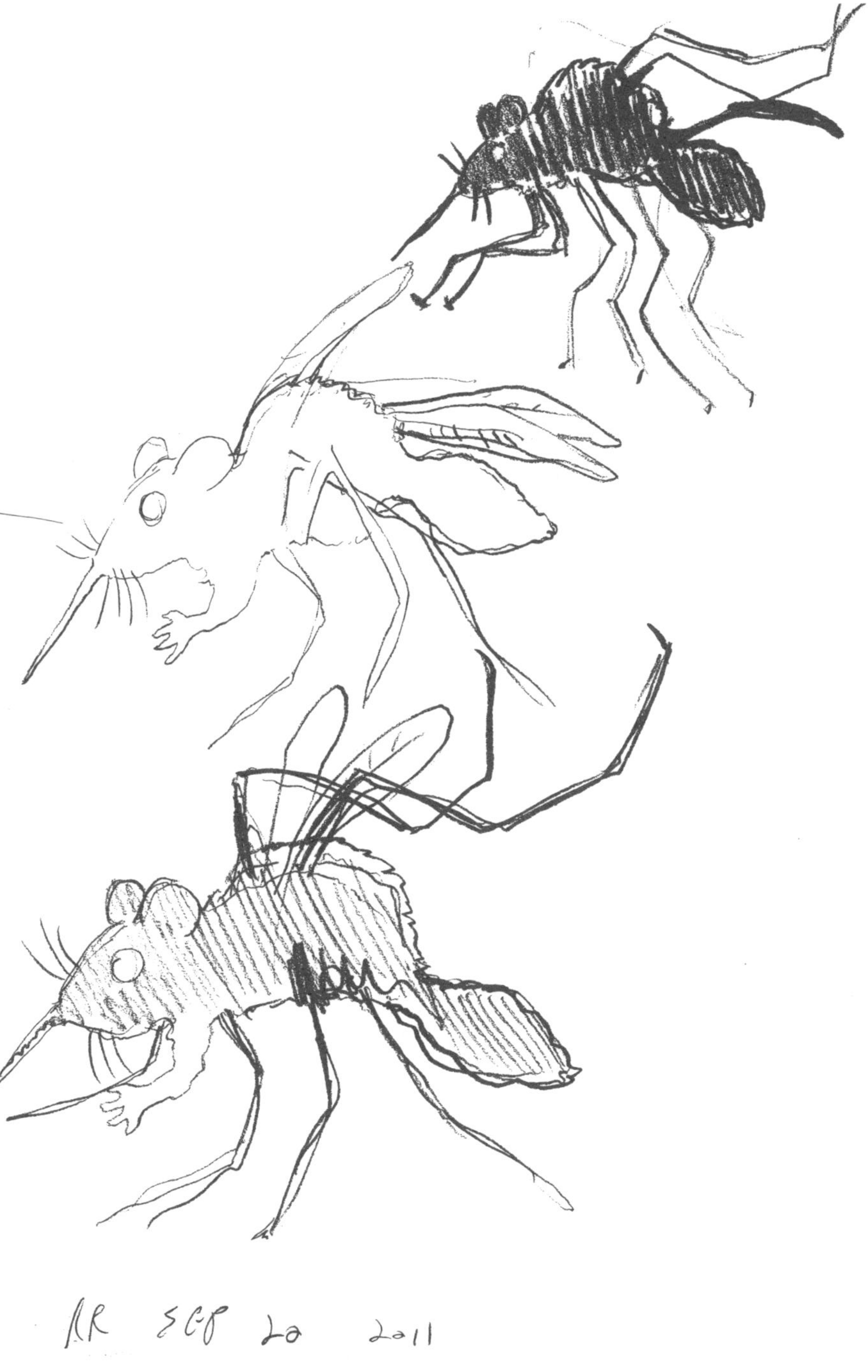
RR SEP 20 2011

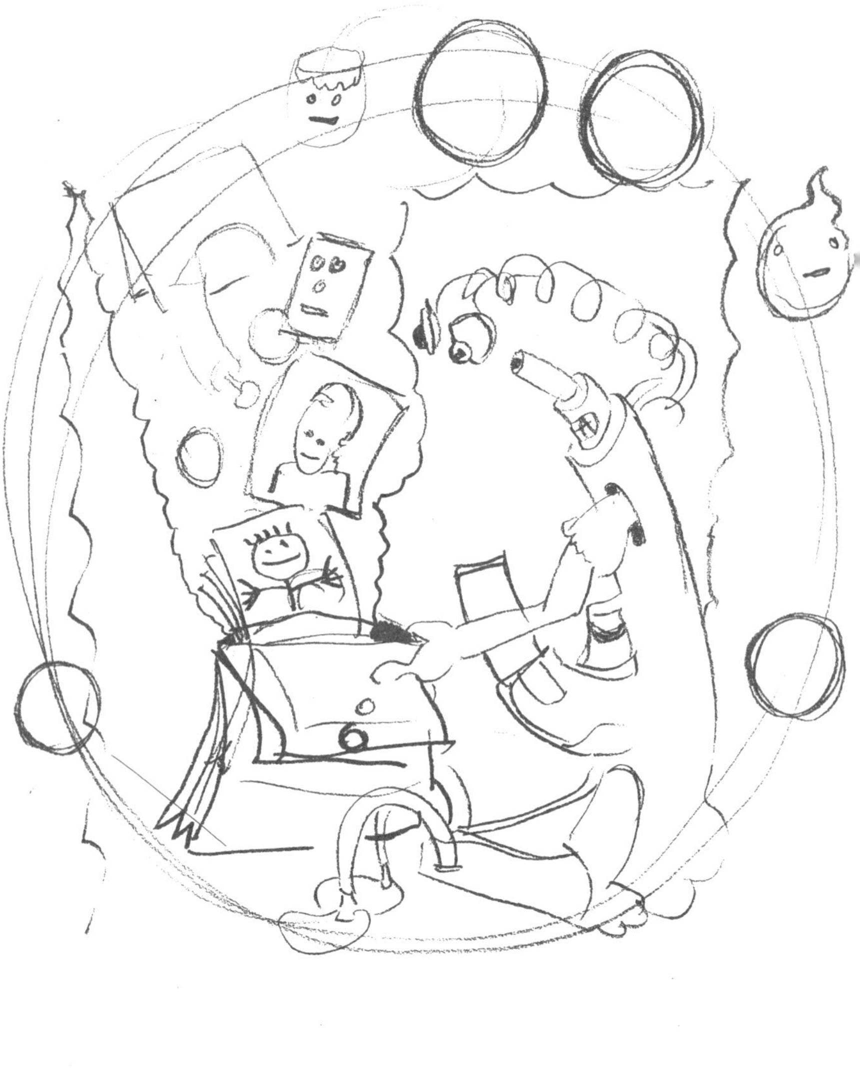

RR oct 1 2011

7 + 18 - Doubled panels (?)

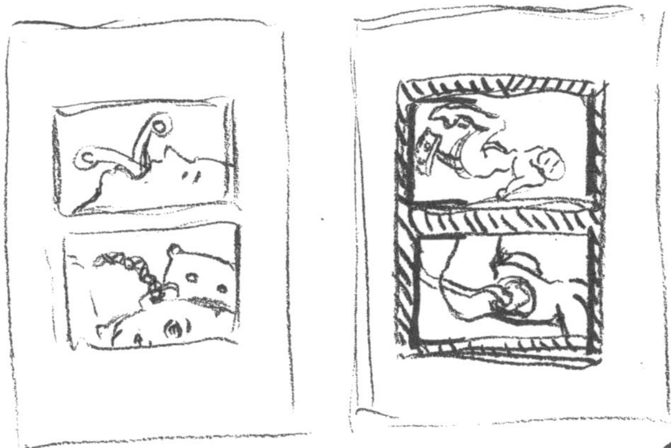

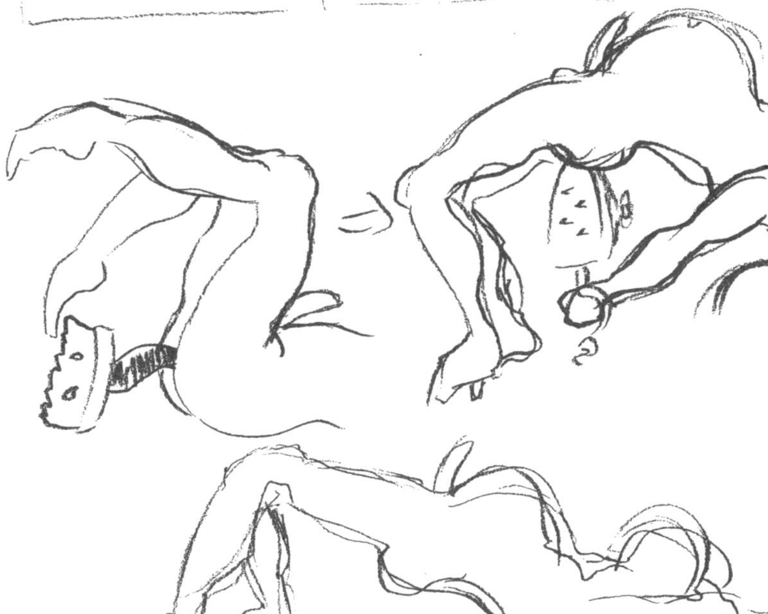

RR, Nov 13th 2011

AR Feb 19th 201
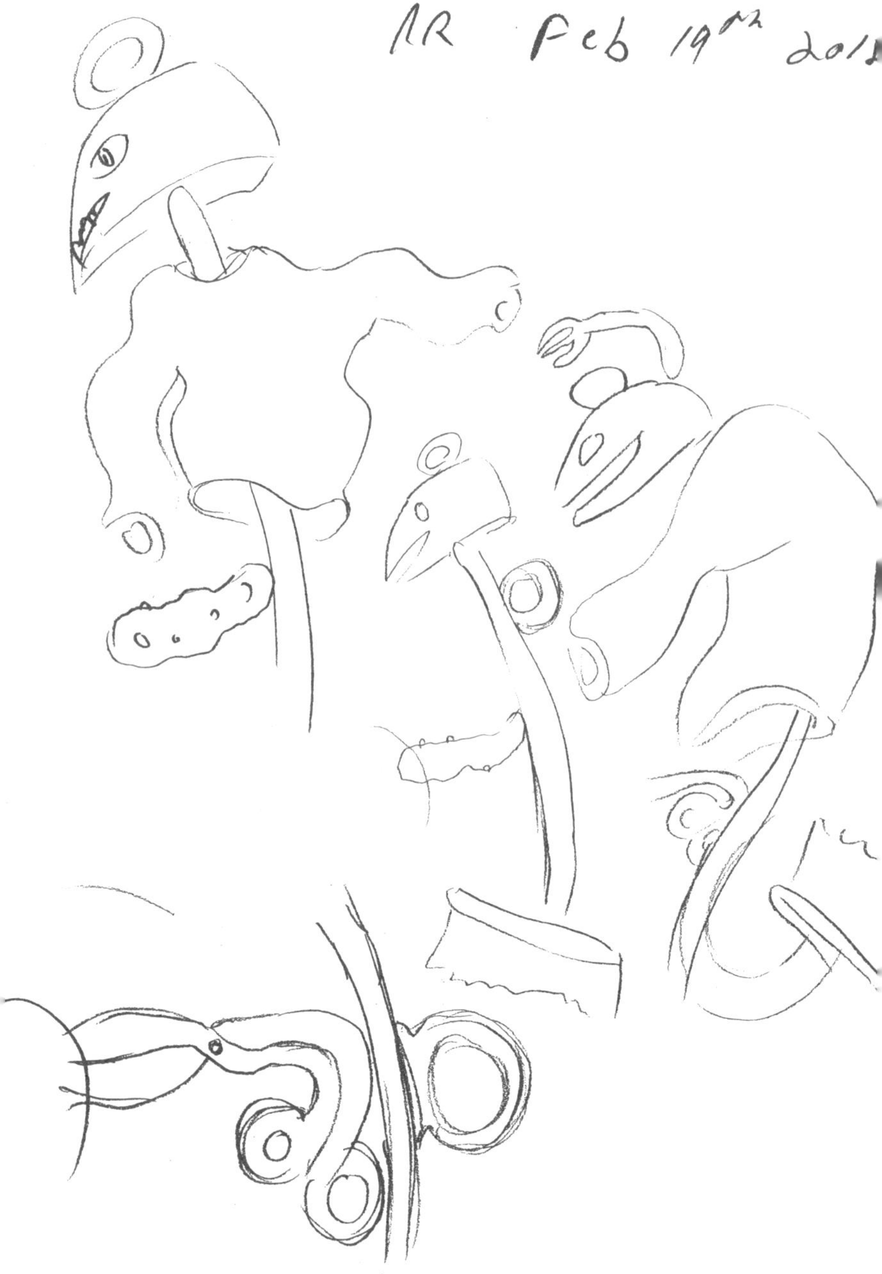

הללה
מתוק

ate 21

(small organ at top might be the gallbladder - but its location at center appears more like an inner-clitoris)

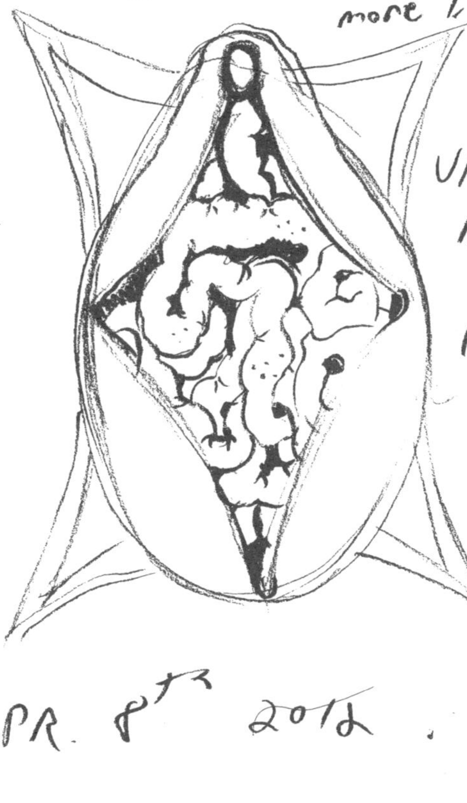

Vladimir's Bowels & Rublev frame

APR. 8th 2012.

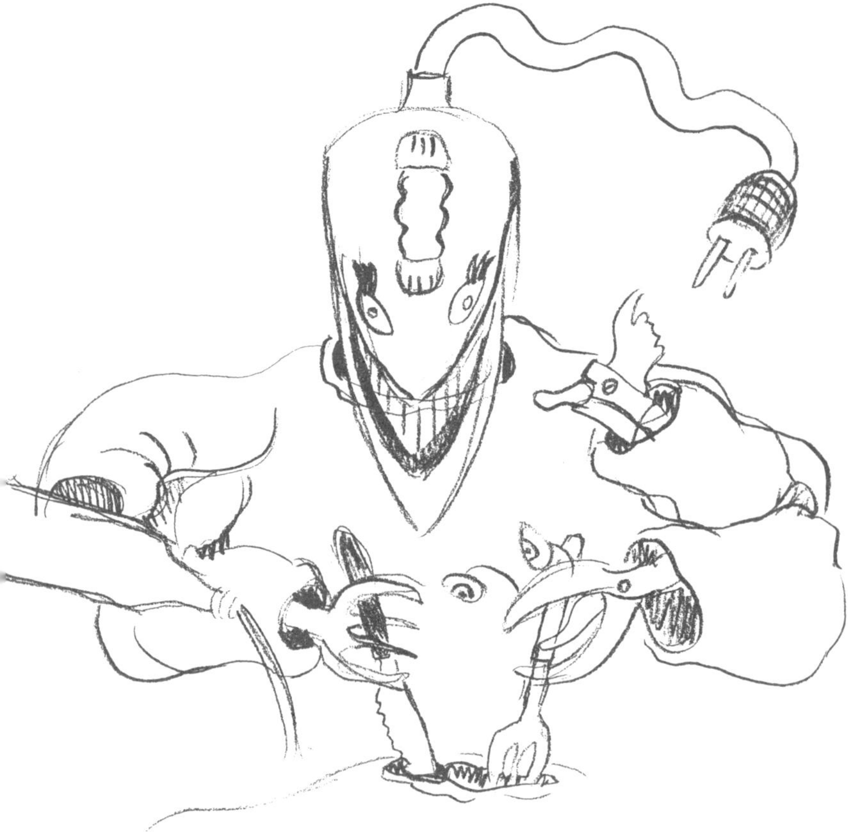

objects feasting on Vladimir
(# 27 – source:
Magritte, Le Sorcier 1951)

CR June 24th 2012

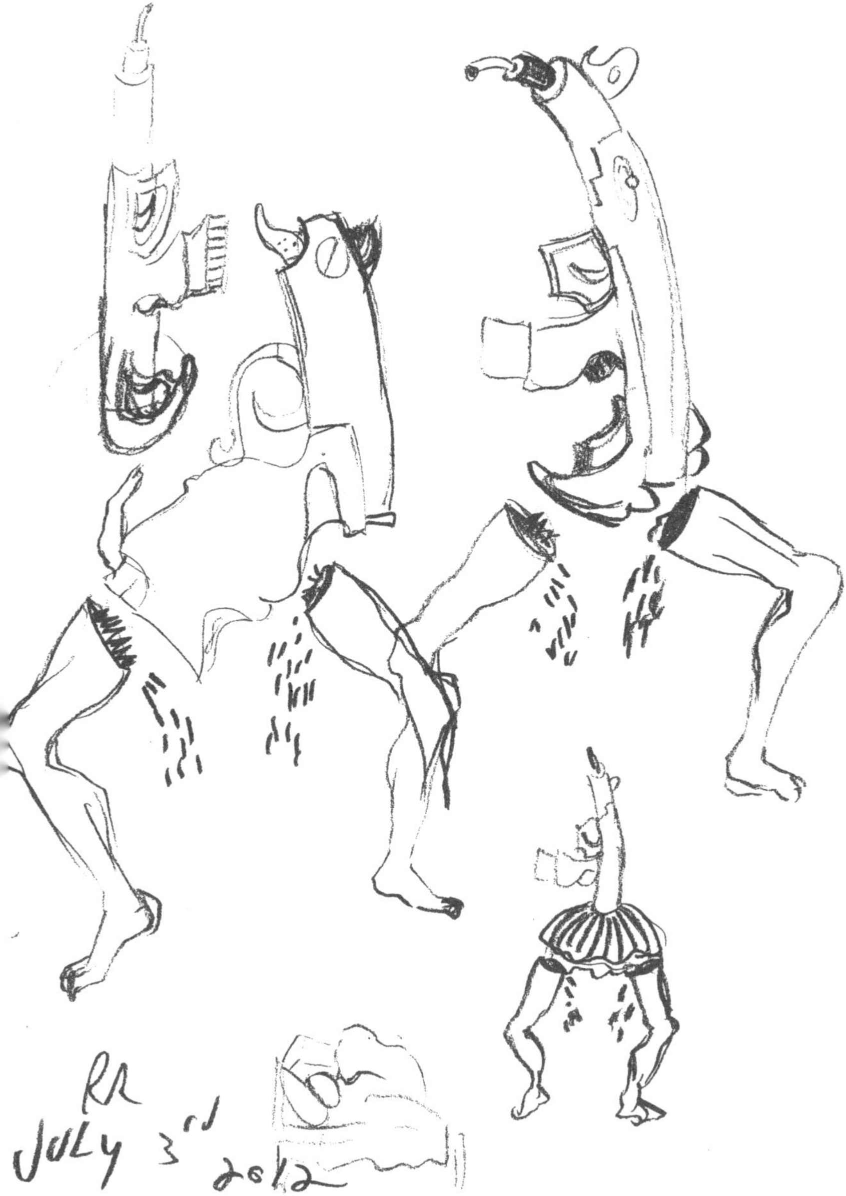
RR
JULY 3rd 2012

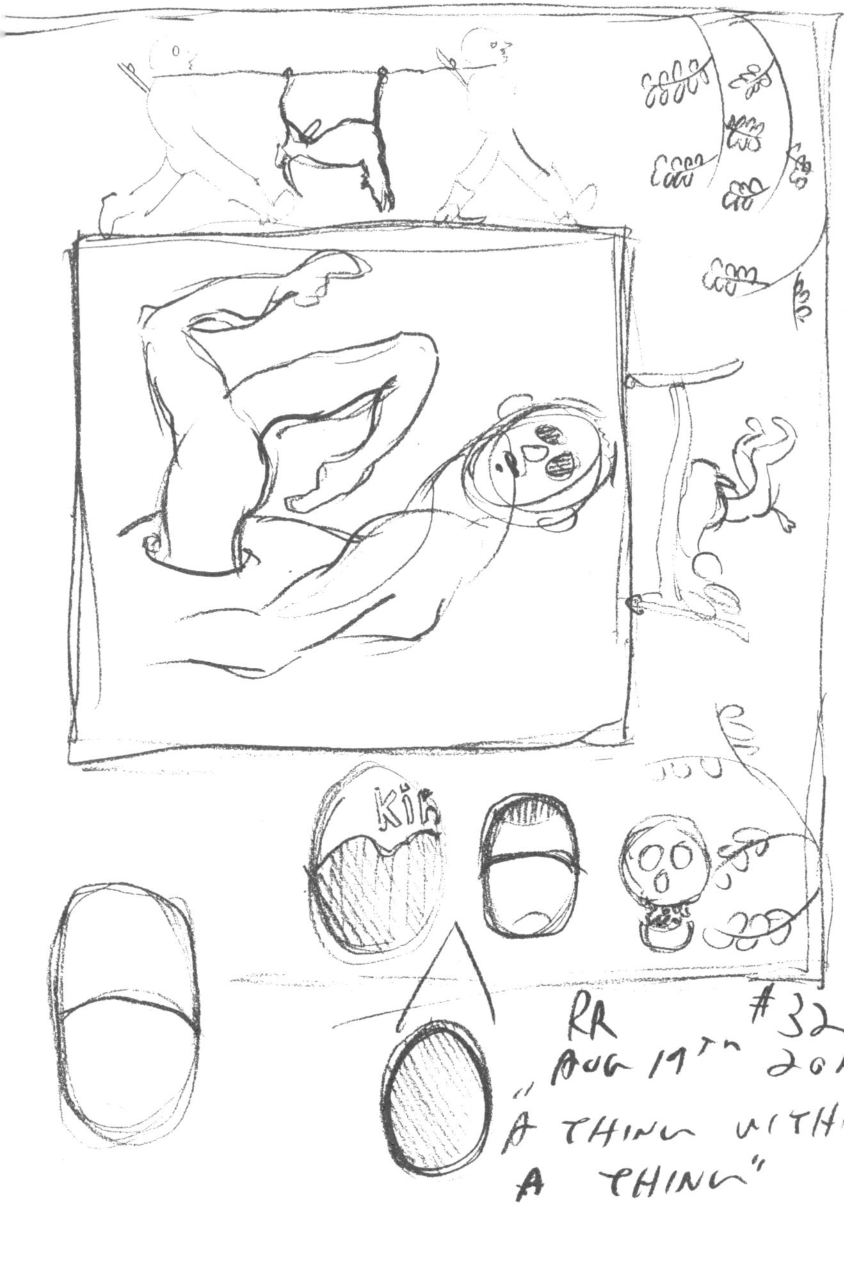

RR #32

AUG 19TH 2012

"A THING WITHIN A THING"

The Dust Files

by Paul B. Preciado

Foreword

In October 2019, the Opportunity, one of the two robots sent to Mars as part of the Mars Exploration Rover in 2003, returned to Earth with a dust sample from the desert of Arabia Terra on the red planet. The dust was initially seen as an object of mineral research and as such was treated as particles of iron oxide. It was not until 2024 that it was publicly revealed that each reddish dust particle contained several nanochips. This generated an overflow of missions to Mars in the desire to collect, possess, and analyze the totality of the desert dust. Yet, dust particles on Mars are as innumerable as the stars of the universe. They say that this immense task will take 20,000 years to complete. Meanwhile, some scientists claim that the earth's deserts should also be placed under scrutiny, since every particle of earthly dust could contain unknown surprises. What if dust is our largest archive?

The full content of the analyzed dust particles from Mars has not been disclosed. But in April 2026, AlgoritAmoR, the Mexican hacking group working on extraterrestrial communication, leaked part of the confidential information found in one of the nanochips called медитация пустыни (meditation of the desert). The documents contained within are commonly known on the internet as "the dust files." The information was codified in an unknown cybernetic language that nevertheless was translated into English; the translation process proved that the texts have connection with modern Arabic, Chinese, Dutch, Hebrew, Oromo, Quechua, Russian, and Spanish. Until now only a small part of the 7,000 billon documents included within the nanochip have been studied.

The Dust Files

The document that I have decided to publish here is part of the first revealed files found in медитация пустыни. It is a fragment of a doctoral dissertation about some earthly events that, according to the document, took place between 2008 and 2019. The dissertation is said to have been written in 2758 by Albertoriam Arralis-12 to obtain a doctorate degree at the University of Amazonis Planitia in Mars. Arralis's research project is mostly concerned with the field of sexology, human biotechnological mutation, and technologies of governance. It is also based on a detailed analysis of a short film written and directed by Roee Rosen in 2016 called The Dust Channel. *It is uncertain why this film retained such value up until 2758 and why it has deserved such a committed study. Why has this film been preserved? Why has it become such an important piece of evidence for researchers of the twenty-eighth century? It is difficult to say, except for the fact that the Dyson DC07, a vacuum cleaner that Rosen's opera centers on, seems to be an "ancestor" of the writer of the dissertation. Moreover, the importance given to dust in the archive and in the museum of the civilizations on Mars might explain the centrality of the document in* The Dust Channel. *It is also possible that what I am calling here Martian civilization is nothing other than the human project of colonization of the red planet which will take place in the future.*

It is inexplicable, at least according to our scientific knowledge of space and time, that something written in 2758 can "appear" to us today in 2026. For some, this time incongruence makes any further discussion invalid. But I disagree, not knowing the complete process should not prevent us from understanding some of its parts. As David Garnett affirmed in 1922, wonderful or supernatural events are not so uncommon, rather they are irregular in their incidence. Thus, there may be not one marvel to speak of in a century; often enough there is a plentiful crop of them. But the strange document which I shall reprint here came alone, unsupported, without companions into a hostile world, and for that very reason it claimed little general attention from the already too delirious humankind. Certainly, its explanation of the facts and our reconciling of them with general notions of the truth is what we shall find most difficult to accept. Yet, what it contains has been fully proven, and not by one witness but by a dozen, all respectable, and with no possibility of collusion between them.

Some of the events described in this dissertation are well known to us. Others have gone by unnoticed, and others have been reconstructed by twenty-first- and twenty-second-century narratives and accounts. I have decided to share the abstract and first chapter of the dissertation and to submit both texts for your consideration with the hope that you might find something to discern about the despicable state of the world at the beginning of the twenty-first century as well as gain some insights into the transformation of humans and their governmental techniques which is to come in the future. I have not made changes or additions to the text. Some lines were missing because of the reconstruction of the nanochips or poor translation. I have left them as they were found. These few pages, these scarce remarks and comments, may not satisfy the most voracious readers, but they might help us to look differently at the engagement with what we still consider humans and machines.

Finally, it is not the question of other times or other spaces that is at stake here. It is rather how we understand desire, fear, purity, kinship, and belonging that is at the core of this document. It is nevertheless impossible to decide if this dissertation has been written by a descendant of humans, a successor of mutant electronic domestic appliances, or an offspring of both. It is up to the judgment of the reader (human or nonhuman) to make such an ethical (and aesthetic) decision.

Paul B. Preciado
Paris, October 17, 2026

Document

Title: *Dysonsexuality, the Building of the Last Human Nation-States on Earth, and the Pleasures of Purity and Race Construction: Roee Rosen's* The Dust Channel *as Case Study* (2011–19).

Dissertation submitted to the University of Amazonis Planitia, in accordance with the requirements for the award of a Doctor of Philosophy, Mars, 2758

Author: Albertoriam Arralis-12
First advisor: Hilaritedt Kauzkious-159
AI advisor: Nomos-AKJJ-X

Abstract

This dissertation seeks to paint a more accurate picture of the political advent of dysonsexuality and the economic, aesthetic, and affective transformations that came with it. We will do so by bringing together late twenty-first- and early twenty-second-century scientific bibliographic data, as well as reflect on the key document on this event: a domestic opera filmed by artist and suspected mutant Roee Rosen in 2016 and called *The Dust Channel*. This dissertation explores the relationship between Marskind and vacuum cleaners through the lens of human and early Marskind narrative productions from the nineteenth and early twenty-second centuries, including Wilhelm Hauff, E. T. A. Hoffmann, Franz Kafka, Ulrike Ottinger, Angela/Hans/Ashley Scheirl, as well as early Marskind authors such as Alcaboile Uyukate. In each reference, the Dyson DC07's name is put to different use. It is, of course, crucial that we remain aware of the fact that this sexual electronic being has evoked such powerful feelings when attempting to write a more value-free account.

Rosen's *The Dust Channel* offers insight into the long-standing tradition of positioning vacuum cleaners as the mirrors of Marskind, which can reflect as well as question our perception of who or what constitutes a Marskind *soulsomaton*. Finally, and based on the centrality of the opera in the film and its influence on post-scientific and discursive works after the 2100s, this thesis shall argue that vacuum cleaners and humans are the ancestors of Marskind, being that their political and psychosomatic techniques are still at work in present configurations on Mars.

Chapter One

Technological Environmental Background and Sex-Political Consequences of Hybridizing Humans and the Dyson DC07: Early Stages

This dissertation is a first account and a post-scientific study of a little commented phenomenon within certain human Earth societies during the first decades of the twenty-first century. Between 2008 and 2019, when the borders of what was then called "nation-states" were the object of intense surveillance to prevent the passage of moving human bodies (named "aliens," "refugees," and "migrants" and treated as a subhuman, dispensable class), it is said that a series of electronic vacuum cleaners called Dyson DC07 bio-mutated and started to have sex with "heterosexual couples," which may mean that they also electro-mutated.

Heterosexuality was, until the 2170s, the name of a low-tech sexual and economic regime promoting sexual and reproductive assemblages composed of what in the old binary regime of sexual difference on Earth was known as male and female human bodies. The Dyson DC07 was an analogical low-tech vacuum cleaner and purifying domestic appliance invented by human and suspected mutant Sir James Dyson and launched in 2001 by Dyson Ltd. It was best known for being the first to use "root cyclone" technology, with seven cyclone funnels instead of the original dual-cyclone design. It was such a worldwide success that by 2009 most humans had the chance to encounter a Dyson DC07 at least once in their lifetime. We shall refer here to "dysonsexuals" to identify the specific sexual and reproductive formations composed by two human heterosexual bodies and a vacuum cleaner.

The Dust Files

Unexpected changes started to occur in extremely dusty areas, such as the desert territories of what was then called Israel and Palestine, where the Dyson DC07 became the ally of colonial humans in their fight for domestic cleanliness and air purification, but also in other desert zones known as North Africa and Mexico. The last human technologies of governance were highly necropolitical, including not only means of persecution, surveillance, and murder of all moving human delegalized bodies (aliens, migrants, or refugees) but also the use of nuclear military weapons and the abuse of carbon energies.

Heterosexual humans confronted the increasing control of their domestic behavior, and in being mentally colonized by visions of external invasion and fear of nonnational bodies they turned to their domestic appliances as new sources of pleasure and purity. Human earthly low-tech sexuality was then characterized by the connection of certain brain reactions and image production with the tumescence of congested and swollen bodily tissues. The anthropoid bodies found an unexpected source of pleasure in having their tissues sucked by the vacuum cleaner or introducing different parts of the Dyson DC07 into their cavities and orifices. Slogans such as "not a single particle of dust would enter into the anal orifice of my love" were significant to this shift. But it was the combination of pleasure and purity, of sucking and hygienics, of family and state control of the body that defined dysonsexuality, and that, we shall claim here, may explain the evolutionary drifts during the last seventy-five years of the twenty-first century as well as the present formations of the soulsomaton of Marskind. Dysonsexuality, we shall claim, was not a sexual practice but rather a biopolitical regime that promoted the colonial expansion of the nation-state and ensured the stability of the apparently heterosexual couple.

Ever since Uyukate published *On the Origin of Mars Life* in 2674, vacuum cleaners (or, to be more precise, purifying machines) have featured significantly in cultural reflections about civilization on Mars and intelligent Marshood. Uyakate was the first to defend the idea that the Dyson DC07 was the nonhuman ancestor of the soulsomaton Marskind. For Uyakate it was through the dysonization of heterosexuality that mutation and evolution arrived. More recently, there has been a notable rise in academic publications from various disciplines addressing the relationship between Marskind and the more sophisticated AI and digital vacuum cleaners and air purifying machines developed during baroque technopatriarchal times.

Sex historian Eleonoreau Mdiati dedicated a whole chapter of the history of technosexuality to the encounter between the Dyson DC07 and twenty-first-century human bodies: "For the history of technosexuality," Mdiati argues, "the introduction of the Dyson DC07 within the heterosexual couple structure represented the advent of an institution of love and sex that improved the impending disaster of the straight family at the end of the twentieth century. Functioning better within the domestic environment than the already too liberated heterosexual woman and assuming both the sucking of dirt and the sucking of sexual organs—both anal massage and clitoral suction—the Dyson DC07 found its ideal place within the almost obsolete structure of the monogamous couple, and became the new best friend in the maintenance of the nation-state, enabling the stability of both of its social units as well as its borders." For

Mdiati, the Dyson DC07 had few of the faults and all of the merits of the colonial pioneer, and as such should be considered as a new mechanic citizen competing with humans in the last nation-states on Earth.

Not all authors have been as flattering about dysonsexuality as Mdiati and Uyukate. Dysonsexuality was deprecated by some of the last members of humanity in the twenty-second century. Even older comments by Thomas Brecher were less optimistic. Brecher was distinctly judgmental about the unforeseeable changes that the Dyson DC07 could introduce to the natural development of families: "Although it is true that the Dyson DC07 has allowed many married couples to prevent disease and other medical problems, keeping both the domestic environment and the sexual act as clean as possible, the Dyson DC07 should not be mistaken as a progressive force in the struggle for sexual health and virtue. It remains impossible to assign any gender to the Dyson DC07, and therefore what naively looks to be an instrument of cleanliness and pleasure can soon become our worst enemy, opening the door to excessive sexual experimentation and trans-imagination."

A few years later Brecher's suspicions led part of the scientific community to codify normal and pathological uses of the Dyson DC07. It was Ronaldi Victorson who first introduced the name "Dysonism" as a pathological sexual practice. For Victorson, those that promoted the introduction of a Dyson DC07 in each and every house of the nation had underestimated the dangers that this cleaning wonder would bring. Victorson called dysonism, "the tendency to have sex with vacuum cleaners and other cleaning, sucking, electronic domestic devices that compromises the reproductive functions of couples and jeopardizes the efforts of the nation-state to reproduce and extend itself up to the confines of the galaxy." He argued that, "the Dyson DC07 should be surveilled and put with the undersexed, the hypersexed, the rapists, the stranglers, rippers, stabbers, blood-sucking vampires, males in female clothes, stuff fetishists dominated by a shoe or a handkerchief, lovers of fur and velvet, slaves of scatology, frotteurs and voyeurs, and the endless army of men who lust after woman in perverse ways but had no desire for her vagina and therefore would never be able to become fathers of the nation. Since the Dyson DC07 has entered the heterosexual bed, the ability to enjoy and perform the sexual act in the normal manner appears to be the most difficult of arts."

It is Franceu Berrios who considered the Dyson DC07 not as a full electronic sexual being but as an external "erogenous zone of the human body," denying legal and political existence to the vacuum cleaners. For Berrios, vacuum cleaners and air purifiers should be treated like aliens, migrants, and refugees, and denied access to the national territory. Accepting a vacuum cleaner into one's own home, let alone into one's own bed, was for Berrios the beginning of the end.

Most human scientific and Martian post-scientific accounts of sexual behavior rest upon evolutionary explanations, rather than attending to the political context and the transformation of technologies of power. Against this tendency, we shall defend here the hypothesis according to which nation-states during the last stages of colonial expansion promoted vacuum cleaners to heterosexual couples to gain control of the domestic environment and to prevent sickness; they also allowed couples to find a new technical connection between their organs. In the last ten to fifteen years, post-scientific research has shown the first mutating symptoms of the human from having experienced the general pleasure of being in relationship with the Dyson DC07 vacuum in the area of Earth 31.5016° N and 34.4667° E.

The last five hundred years of human organization before its mutation were characterized by the proliferation of political regimes that equated racial purity with citizenship, recognizing only the rights of a human body in a certain territory if they could prove their lineage to the place or if they had a certain skin color. As opposed to the liberal idea of the individual as agent of the free market, the last stages of human societal development made family values and sexuality pivotal for a purified nation-state. The stability of such human nation-states seems to have laid upon the alliance between the technoscientific industry and its corporations and the archaic feelings of belonging and supremacy. It is within this aim of purification that the Dyson DC07 became not only instrumental but technopolitically constitutive of the regime: it came to occupy a central role within the neuronal and pleasure production system of heterosexual couples used as colonial units at the edge of the national border. It could be argued that the sexual assemblage with a Dyson DC07 jeopardized the biopolitical aims of the colonial extension. This would have been the case if this kind of human-machine activity had not produced unpredicted results. The encounter of the Dyson DC07 within the heterosexual nation-state family unit was a sexual success in terms of pleasure and identity production, but what was accomplished in terms of an invention of a political technique was more important than simple sex. It was this very assemblage that allowed new generations of dysonsexuals to better understand and refine the colonial strategy taken from the deserts of Palestine and applied to the deserts of Arabia Terra on Mars.

It is our contention that Roee Rosen, probably one of the first descendants of a human–vacuum cleaner reproduction process, was commissioned by the first generation of Marskind inhabitants to create a laudatory opera in order to witness and honor the foundational moments of the dysonsexual evolution. Nevertheless, it still has not been established if *The Dust Channel* can be considered a hymn or if it should be described as a mockery of the colonial and dysonsexual power of the human national regime.

Bibliography

Arendt, Hannah. *The Origins of Totalitarianism*. New York: Harcourt, Brace, and Co., 1951.

Burdekin, Katharine. *Proud Man*. New York: Feminist Press, 1934.

Darwin, Charles. *The Descent of Man and Selection in Relation to Sex*. London: John Murray, 1871.

DSM-5 Guidebook: The Essential Companion to the Diagnostic and Statistical Manual of Mental Disorders, 5th ed. Arlington, VA: American Psychiatric Association, 2013.

Dyson website, www.dyson.com.

Ellis, Havelock. *Psychology of Sex*. London: William Heineman, 1933.

Garnett, David. *Lady into Fox*. London: Chatto & Windus, 1922.

Huxley, Aldous. *Brave New World*. New York: Harper & Row, 1932.

Kafka, Franz. "A Report to an Academy" (1917). In *The Metamorphosis and Other Stories*, translated by Willa and Edwin Muir. Harmondsworth: Penguin Books, 1961.

Kinsey, Alfred. *Sexual Behavior in the Human Male*. New York: Ishi Press International, 1948.

Krafft-Ebing, Richard von. *Psychopathia sexualis*. Stuttgart: Enke, 1886.

Magnus, Albertus. *De animalibus libri XXVI*, 1258.

Mars Exploration website, www.mars.nasa.gov/index.cfm.

Mbembe, Achille. "Necropolitics." *Public Culture* 15, no. 1 (2003): 11–40.

Nabokov, Vladimir. *Lolita*. Paris: Olympia Press, 1955.

Rousseau, Jean-Jacques. *Discourse on the Origin and the Foundations of Inequality among Men*, 1755.

Sapp, Jan. *Beyond the Gene: Cytoplasmic Inheritance and the Struggle for Authority in Genetics*. New York: Oxford University Press, 1987.

Weinbaum, Stanley. "A Martian Odyssey." *Wonder Stories* (July 1934).

Storyboard, *The Dust Channel*, 2016

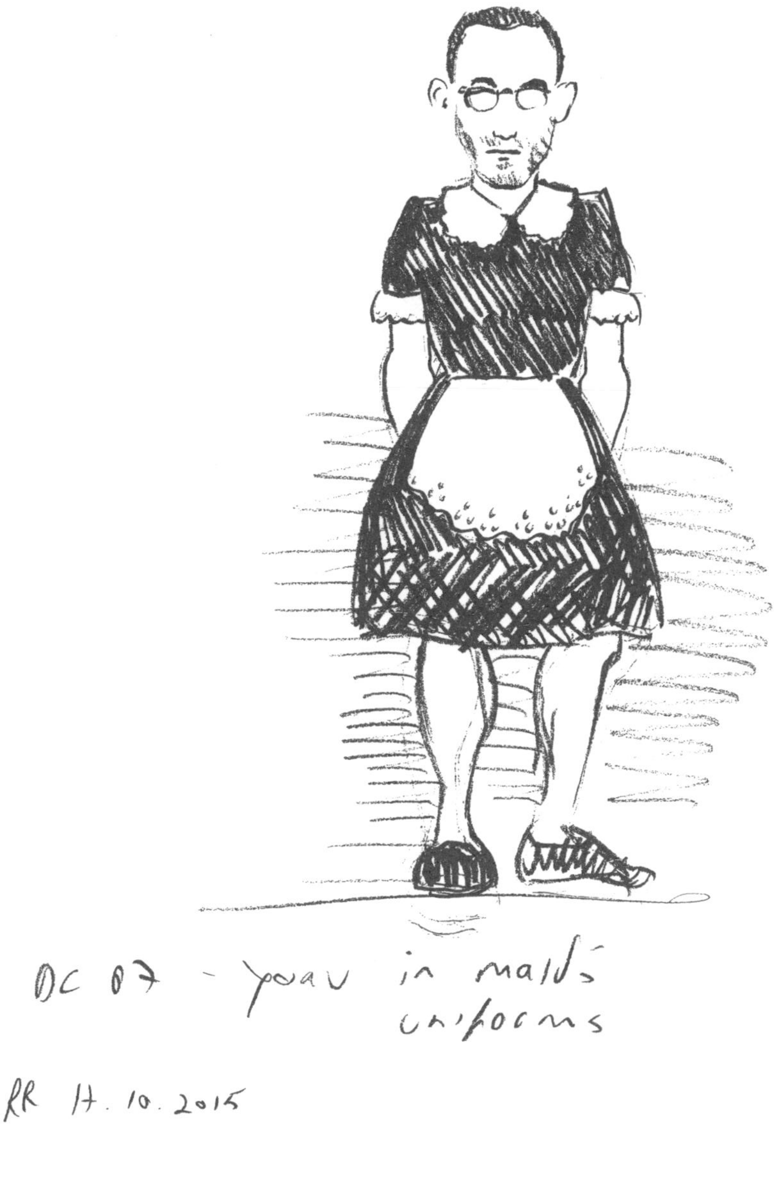

DC 07 scenes 2-3

RR 15.12.15

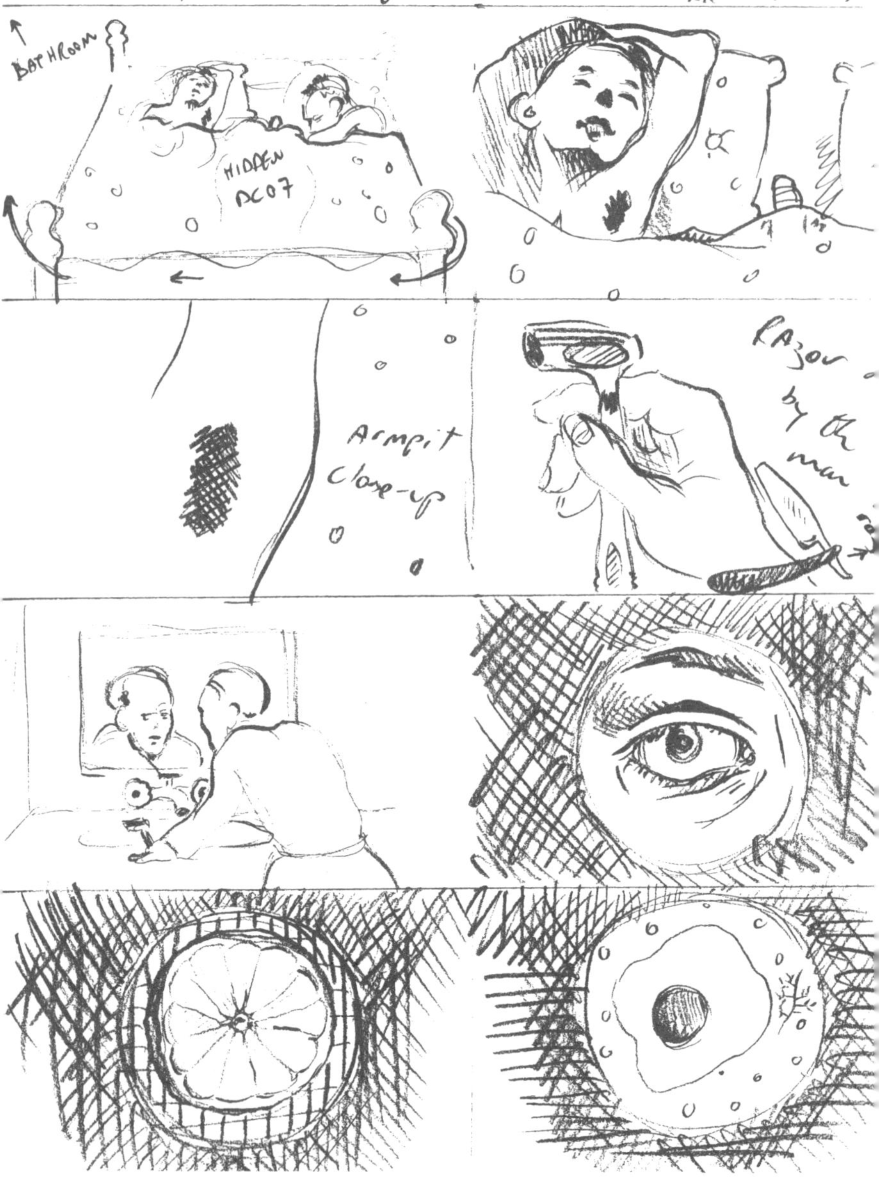

DC 07 Scene 17 AR 16.10.15

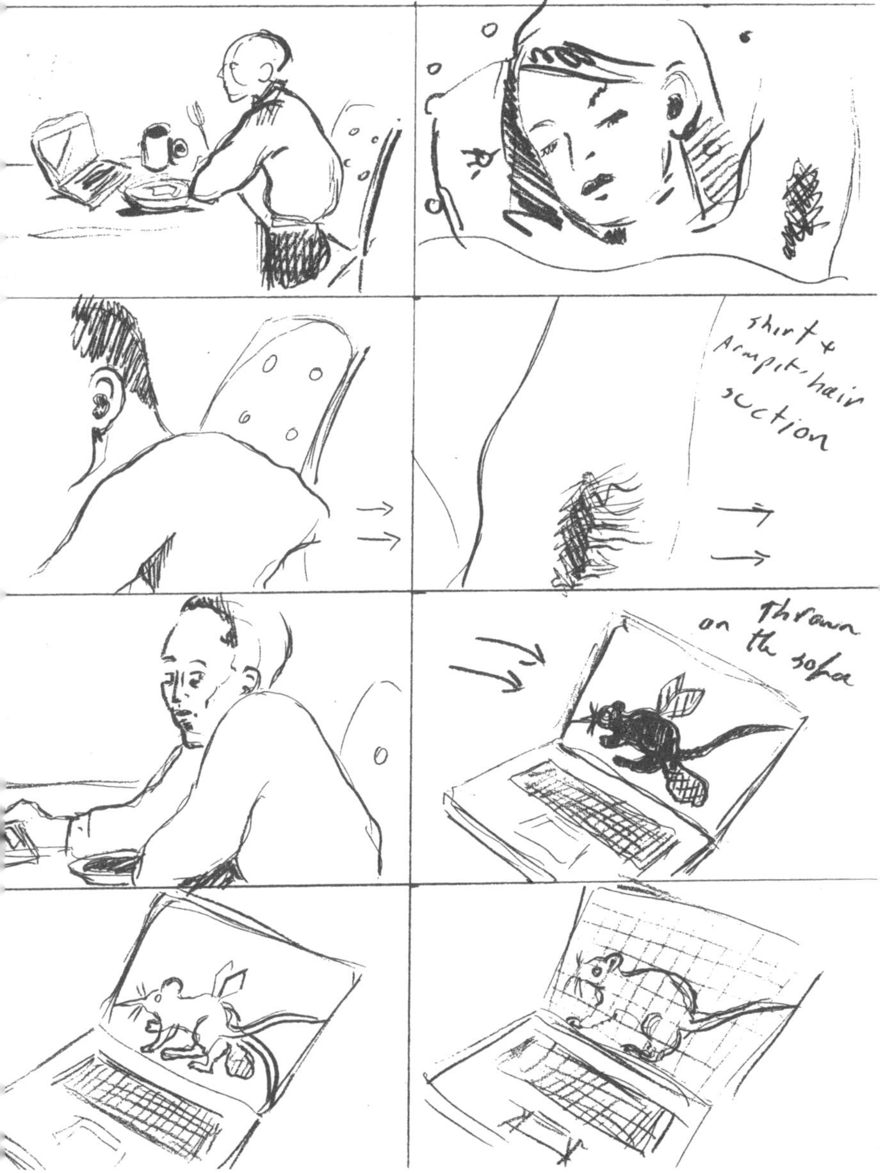

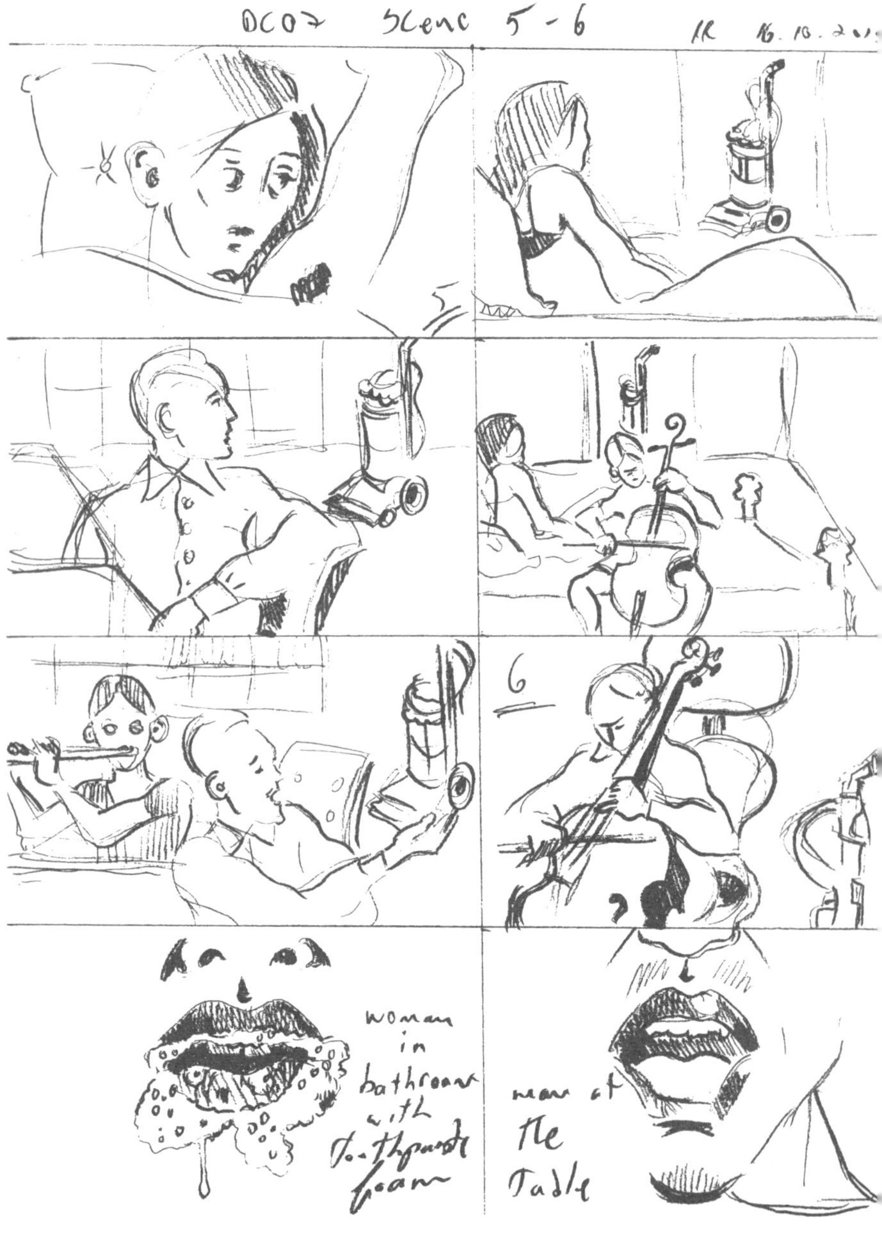

DC07 Scene 5 - 6
IR 16.10.201
5
6
woman in bathroom with toothpaste foam
man at the table

DC 07 Scenes 7-8 RR 17 16. 15

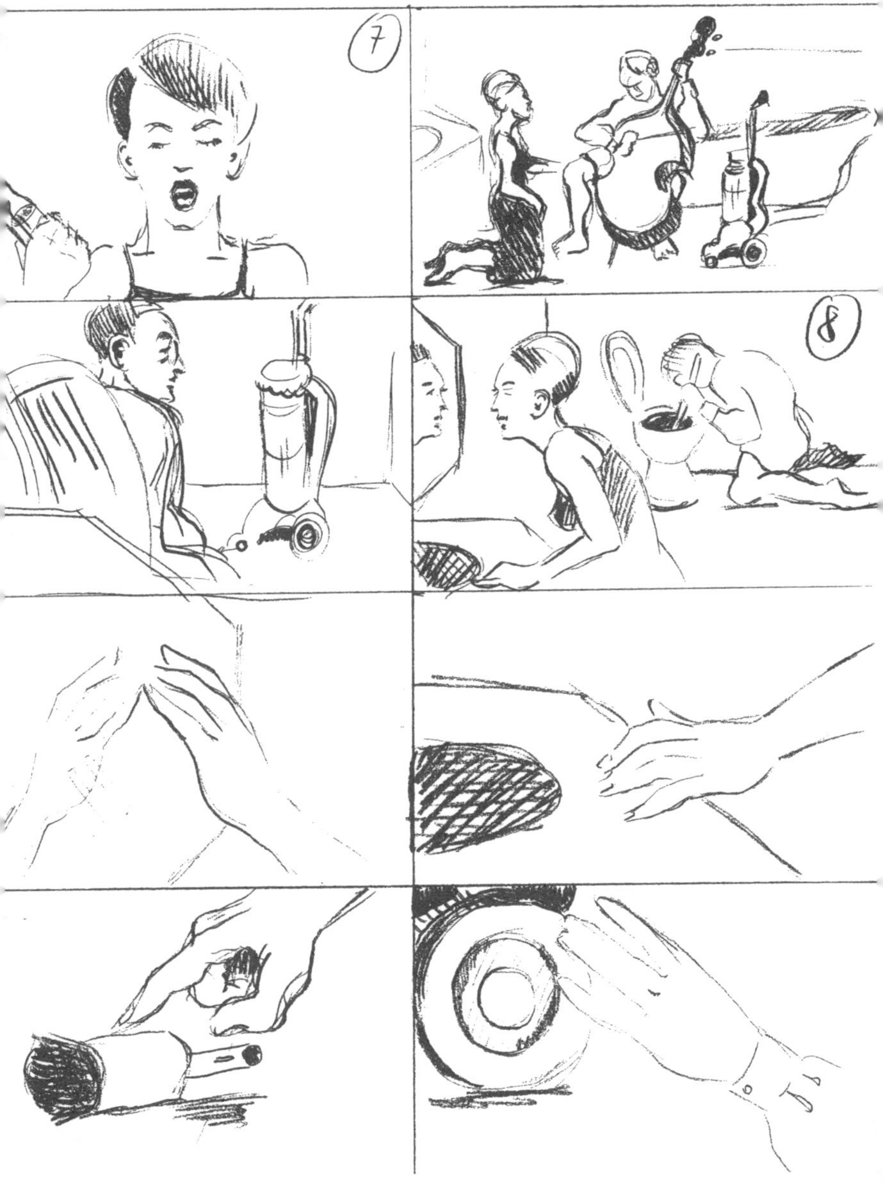

PC07 Scene 9

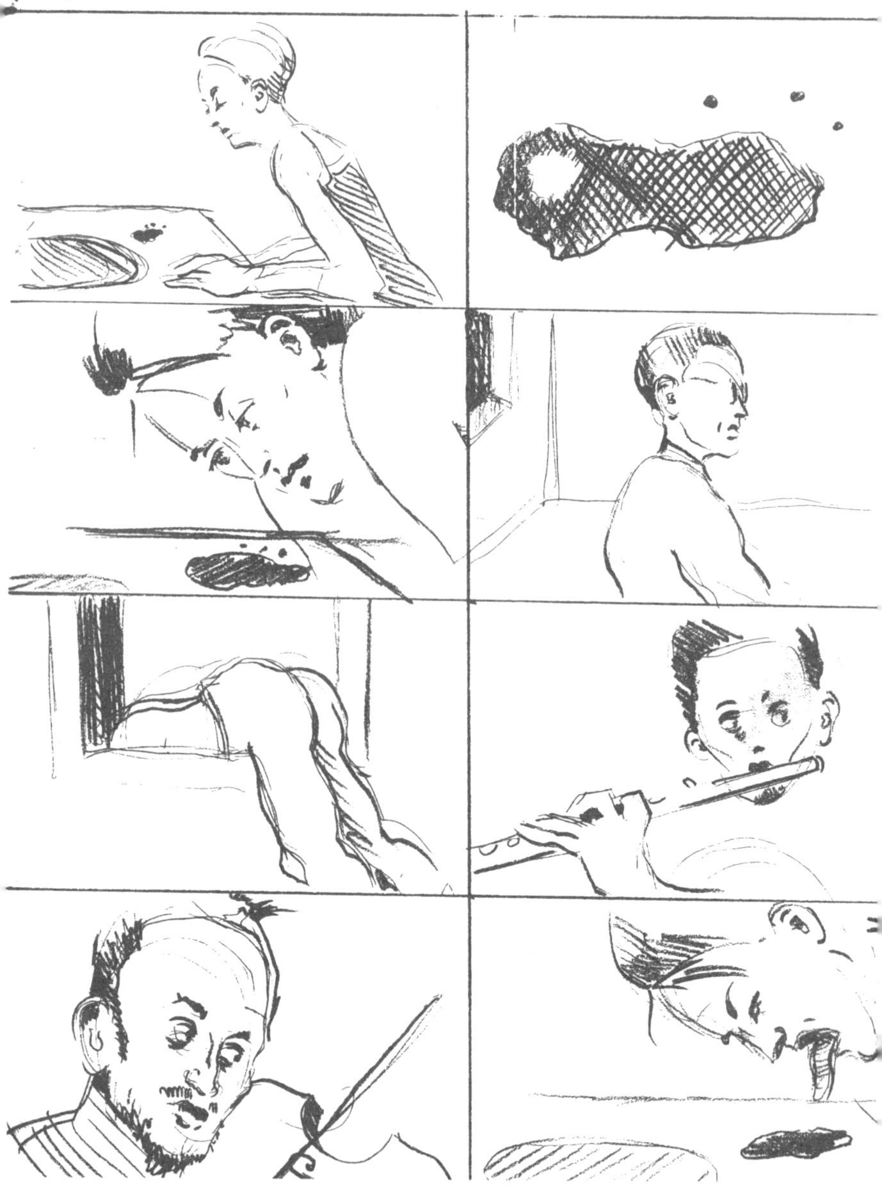

c07, scenes 10–11 16 sep. 19 2015

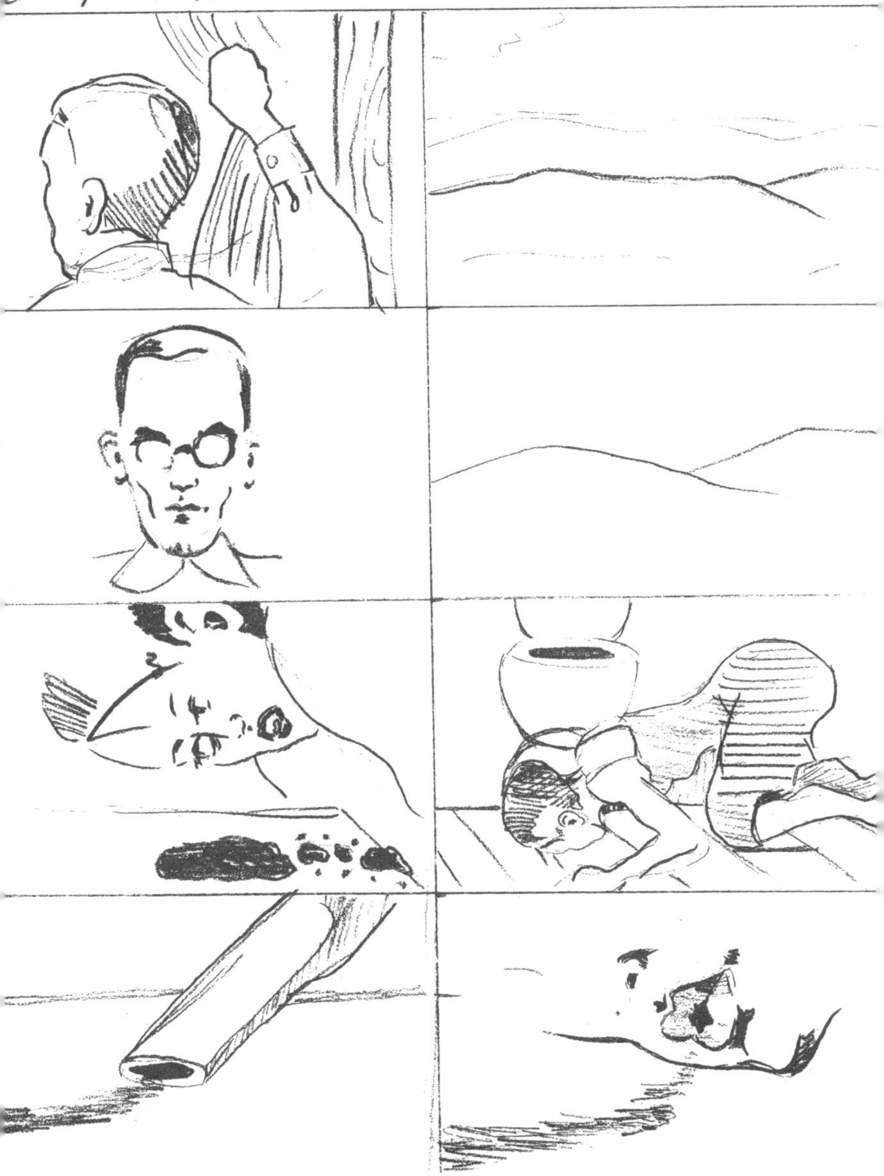

DCO7 scenes 12-13

AR sep 19 '15

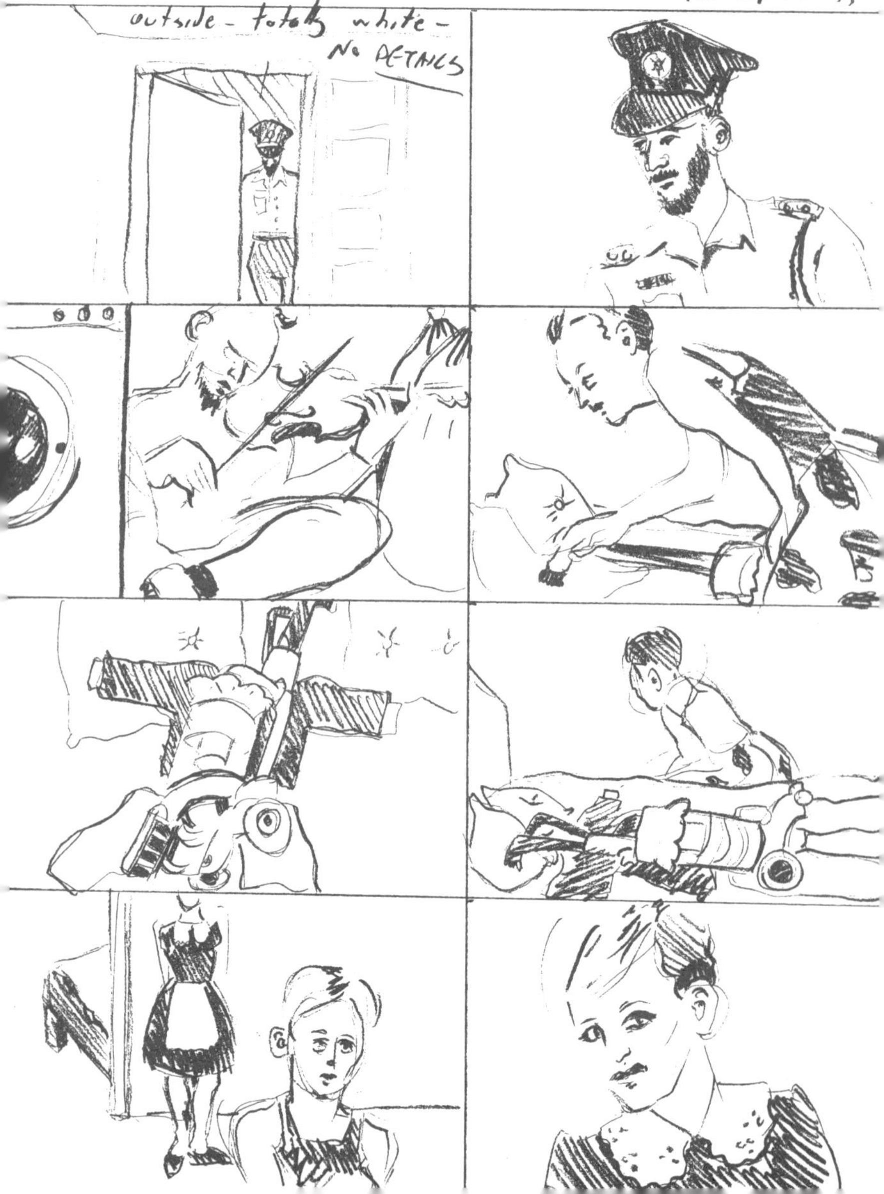

DC07 scene 14 RR sep 21 15

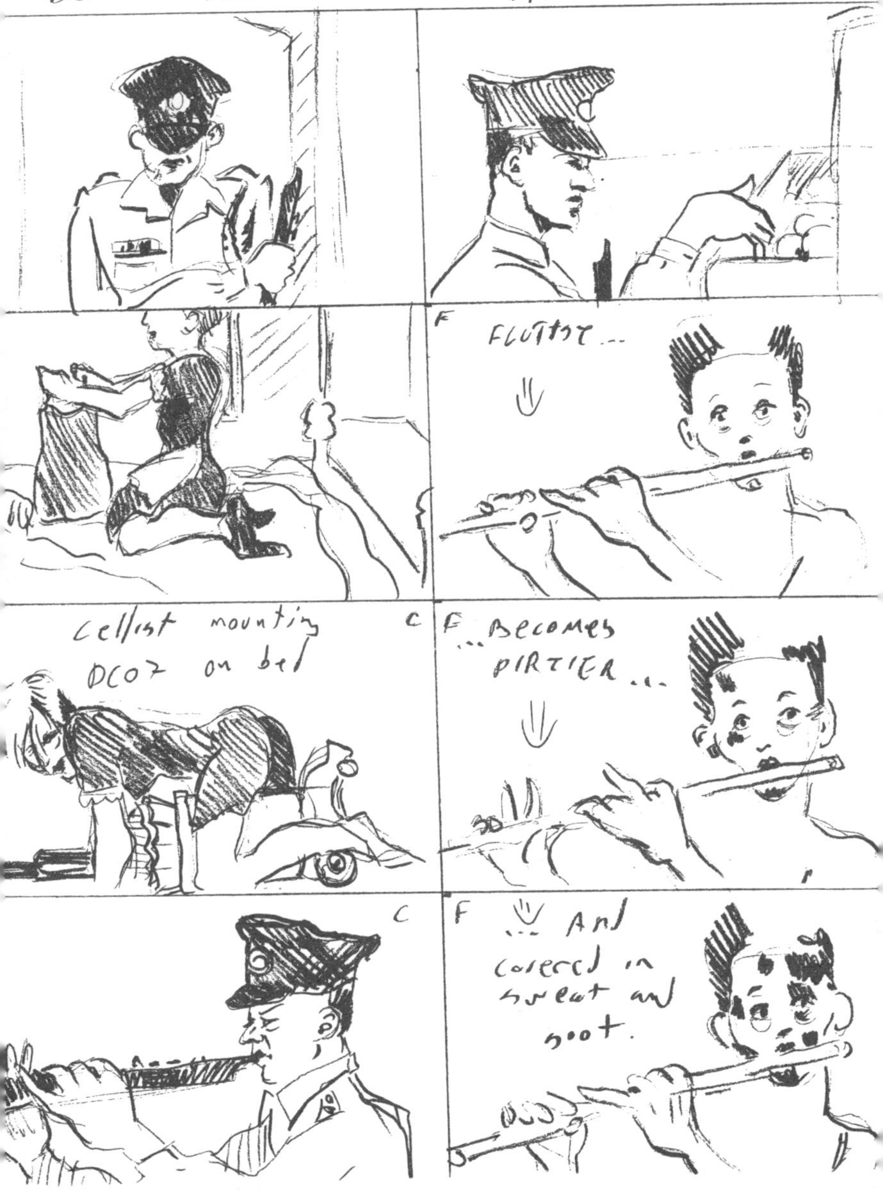

PC 07 Scenes 15-16 RR 22.9.1

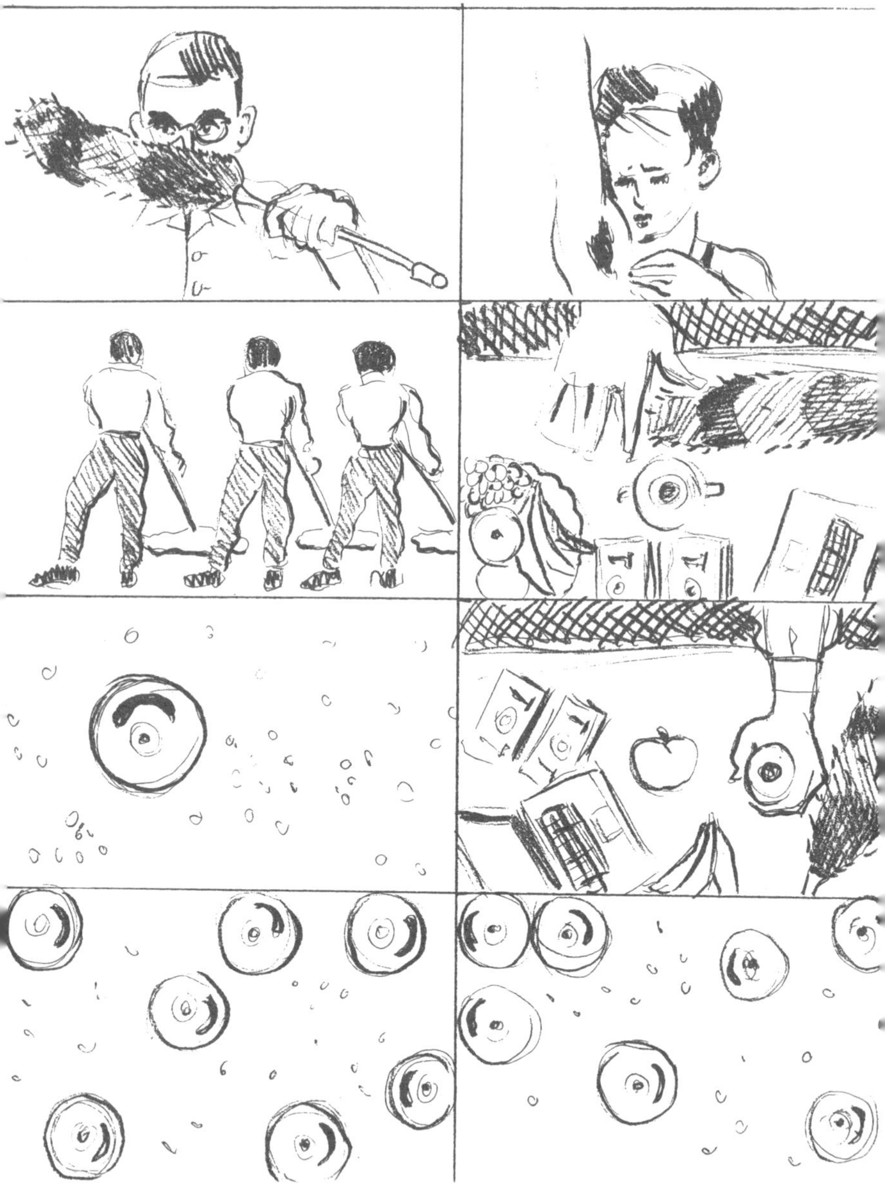

DC07 Scenes 17-18

RR 22.9.2015

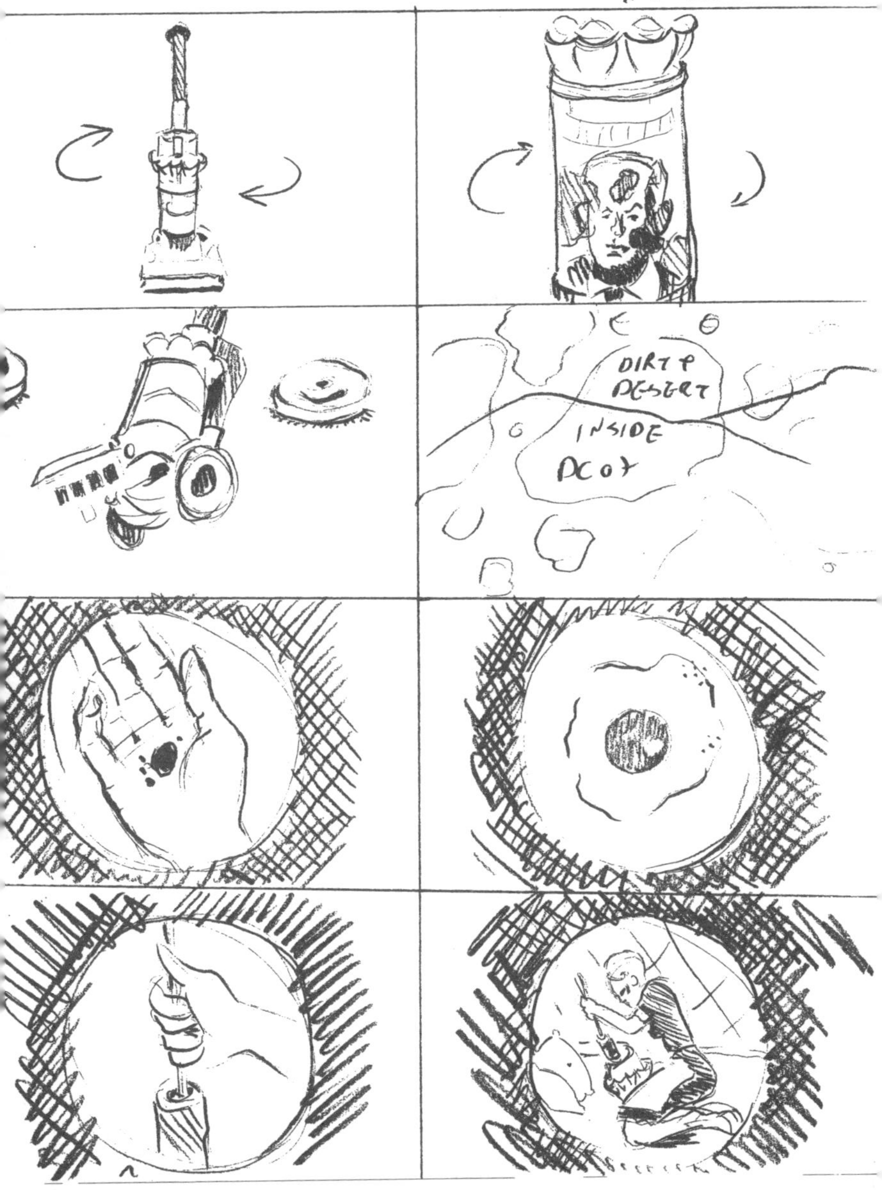

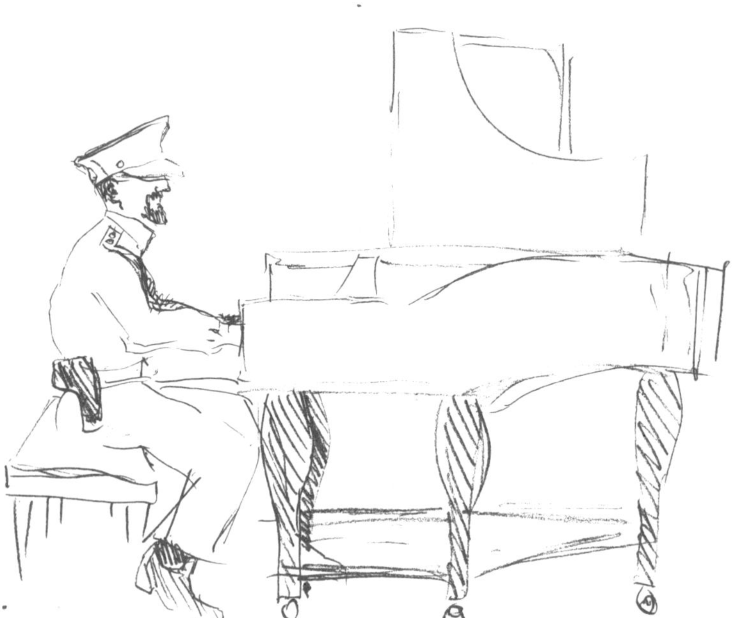

policeman playing the harpsichord
(DCa7, UdI)
RR. Aug 17

BC07 19

sep. 23 15

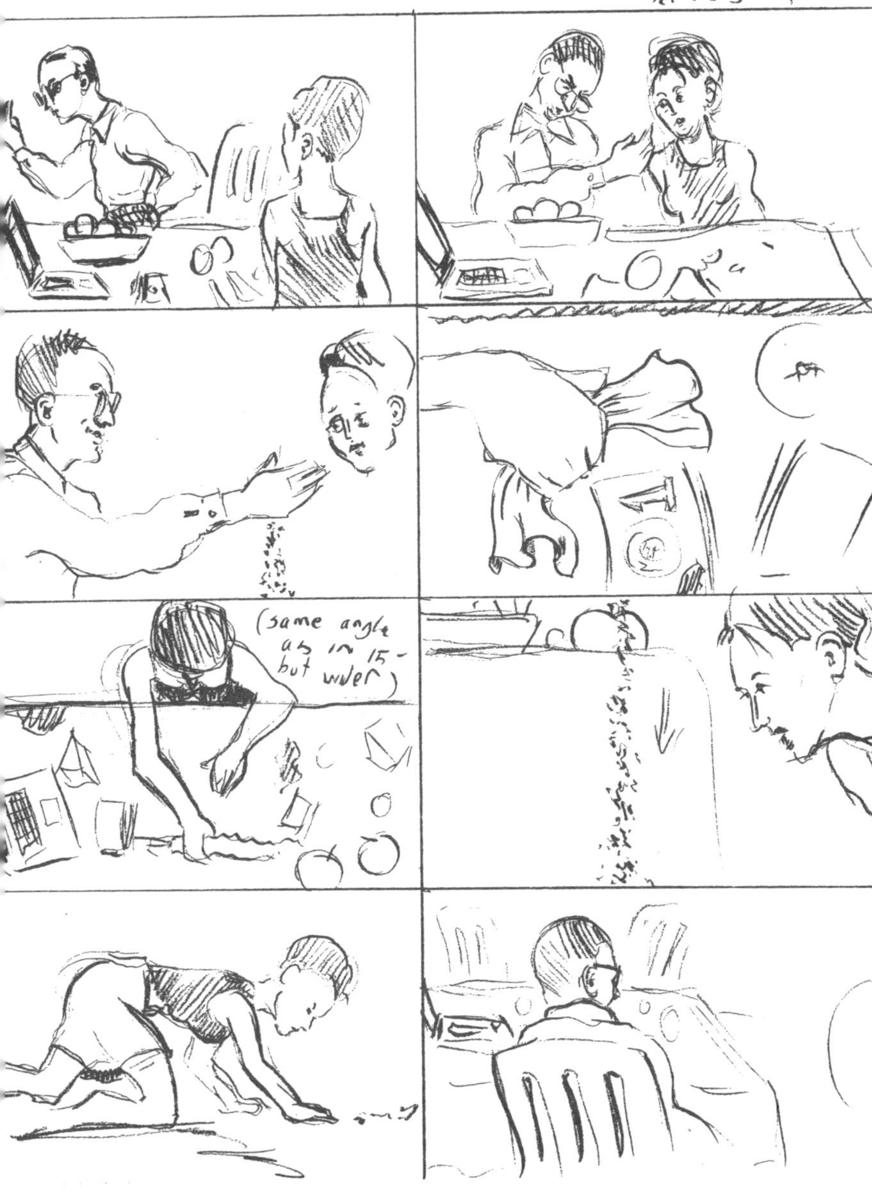

DC 07 20-21 (start) AR SEP·23 '15

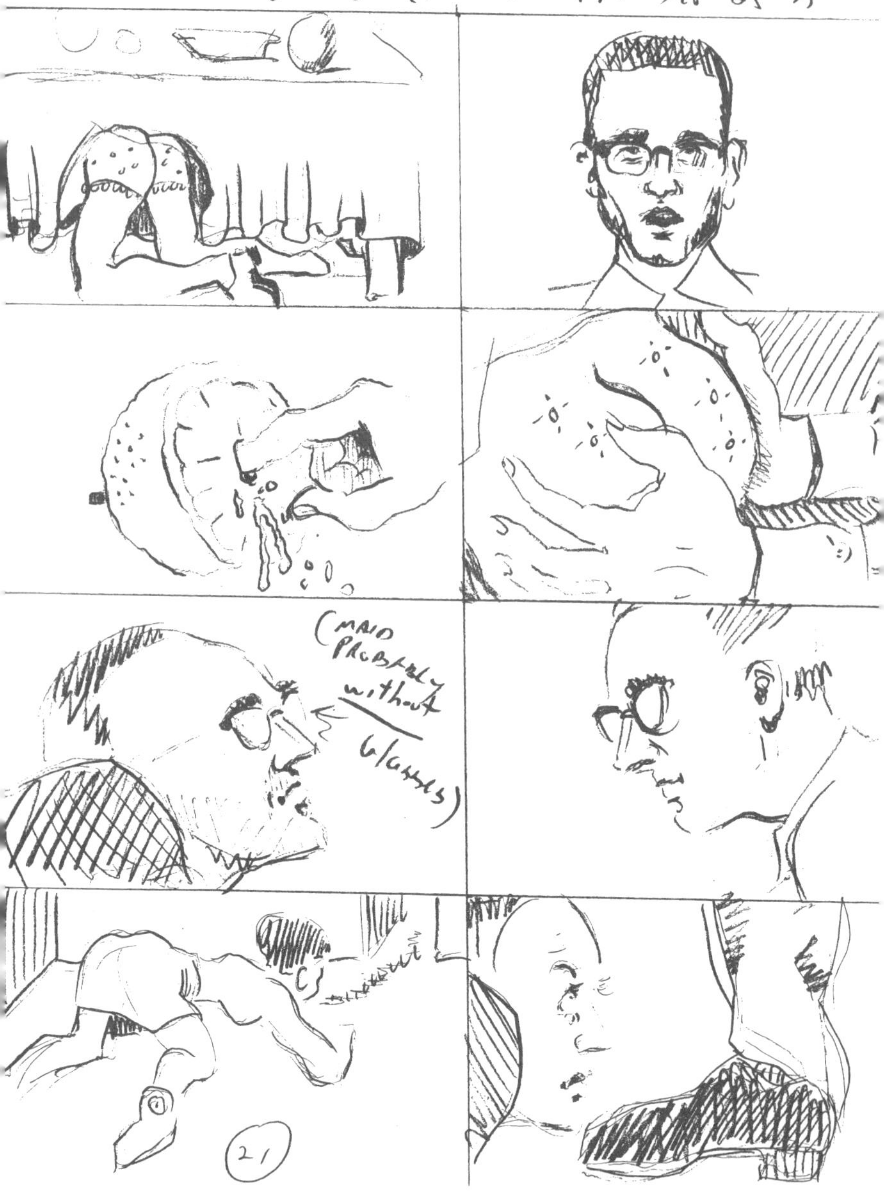

DC 07 21 (cont.) AR Sep. 24 15

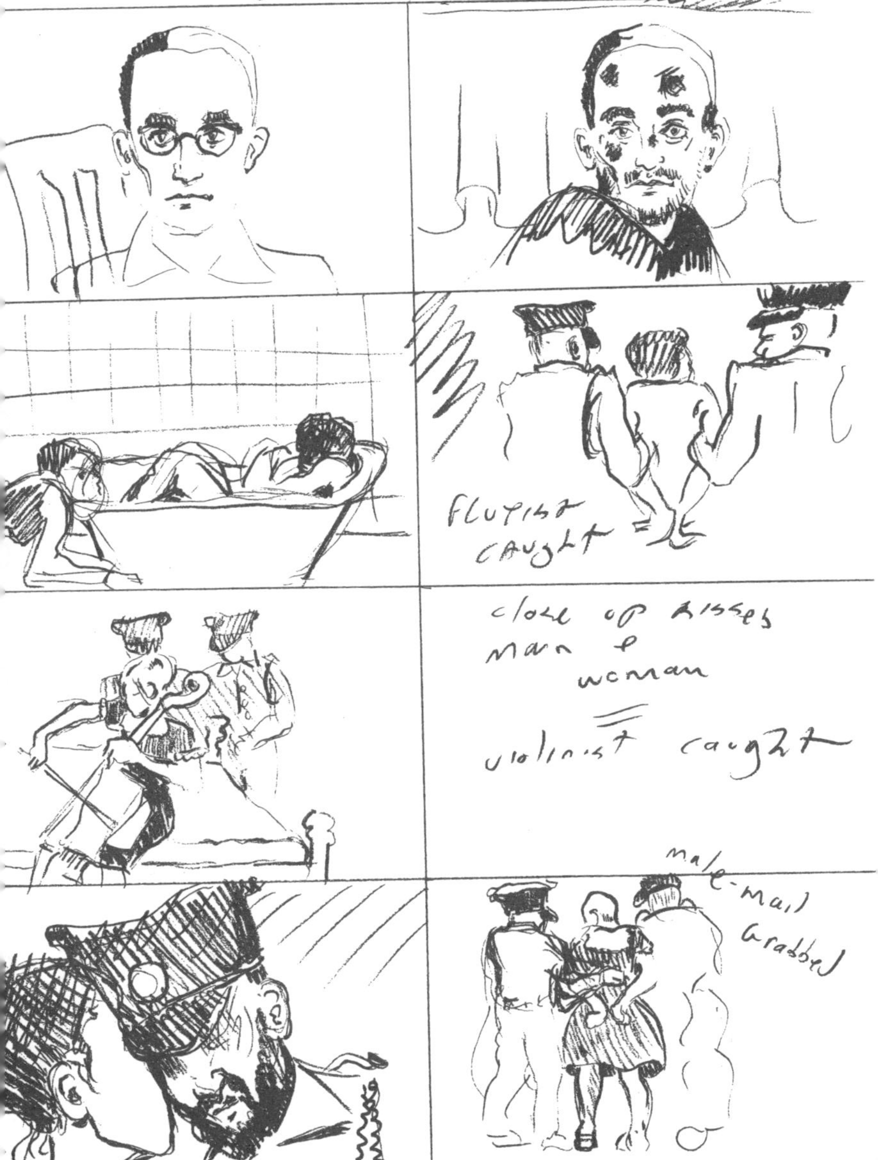

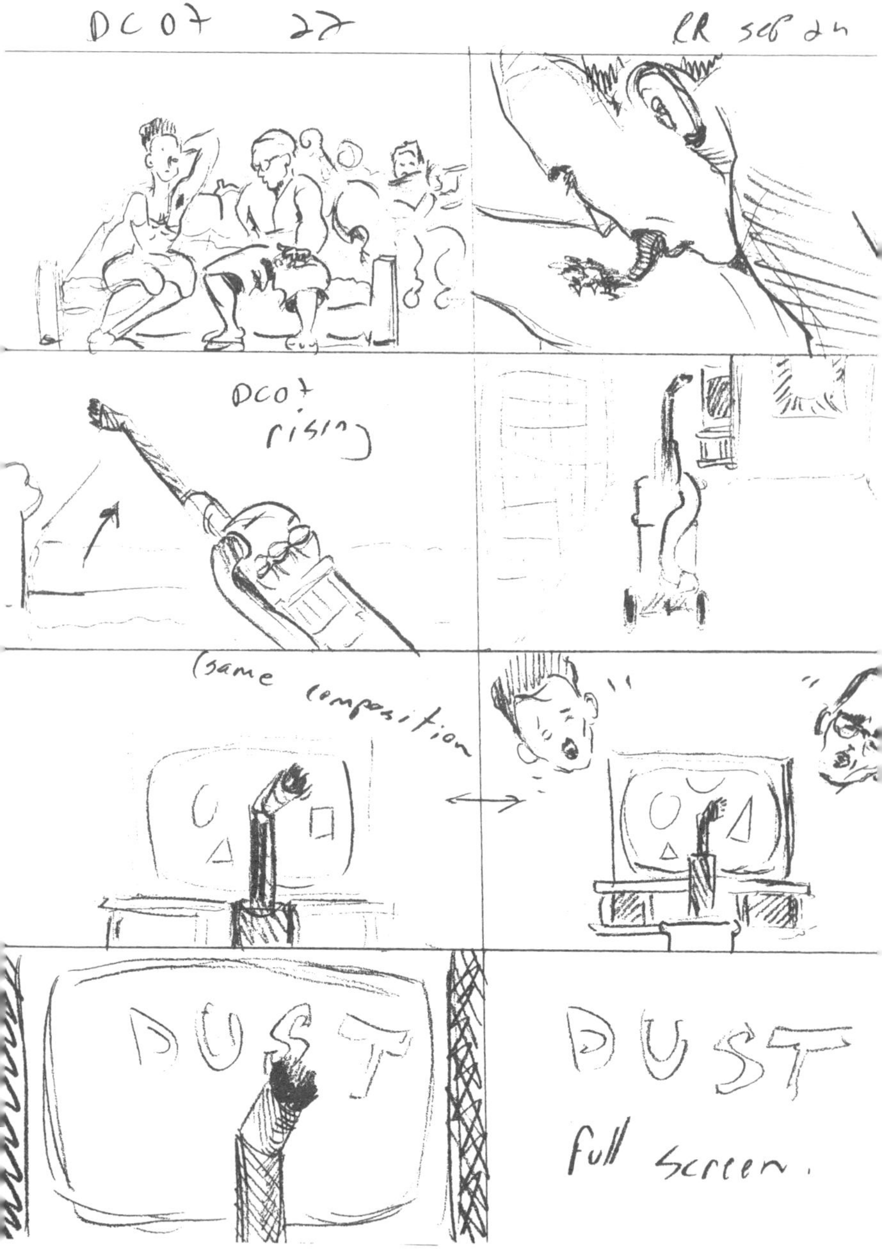

DC07 27
DC07
rising
(same composition
DUST
DUST
full screen.

The Buried Alive Manifesto

by Maxim Komar-Myshkin, 2004

1. We were born into the great cannibalistic Russian culture during the carnivorous era of communism. Later on, Russians found other ways of eating themselves up. We then left that bloody turf.

2. We left our bloody land for an entirely different bloody land. We landed in the oriental Jewish State, mostly because it would let us slip in. But that place demanded us to change, to transform, to evolve, to learn a new language and accept new values – to assimilate. How ridiculous! We disavowed our identity, sure, yes, of course – but we have no intention of assuming another!

3. The global village? America? Zionism? All are foul folly! The only thing this Middle Eastern lot has going for itself is the warm weather.

4. We shall write, create and perform only in Russian. Our films, plays, songs and paintings will ignore what surrounds us. Let there be no mistake: we hate Russian culture, thus we hate ourselves. But our hatred is democratic and universal: we believe all societies equally deserve our hatred.

5. We are living Russian corpses, a pack of spiritual zombies. We intently buried ourselves in the Middle East, but we are still living our Russian past. We are *the Buried Alive.*

6. We live in our secluded grave, equipped with water resistant shutters, acoustic walls and whole cupboards crammed full of products and substances. We take what we need from the outside, so as to go outside as little as possible. The grave aims for self sufficiency, for we shall never trust

the communities around us. We are willing to receive payments for whatever reason, but we hold no wish for company, thank you.

7. We shall never trust anyone who says "we," for we witnessed how vile each "we" becomes once a "we" has any power. Thus, saying "we," we do not trust ourselves.

8. Our grave is a ghetto, our ghetto is a gallery, our gallery is a grave.

9. We are the descendants of earlier packs of inconspicuous people, secretly producing in underground autarchies. Our grandparents: Oberiu; our parents: The Moscow unofficial artists.[1] We inherited the gifts of surreptitious spectacles, hidden performances, silent sound.

10. But we are different than these glorious ancestors. They forged their poetry coffins and art graves as a form of defiance, sovereignty and liberation. But we were not buried alive by others. We freely imprisoned ourselves in our grave. Thus, we have no emancipatory hope or liberating vision, and we certainly cannot offer any to others.

11. Our ancestors imagined themselves emancipated through art. Our ancestors, through their despair, saw a horizon ahead of them. Our ancestors imagined futures when imagining futures was still possible. We no longer possess a sense of a future. We know all too well how old and stale the future is. Nothing ages as grotesquely as the future.

12. Being that we are living our deaths, our future is behind us. We thus always look behind. Our future is the past. We look backward, to the past, for our upcoming actions. We search the past for trends, innovations, fashions and merchandise. The garbage is fresher than the products on the shelves.

13. For us, the piles of rubble that are the past are dynamic compared to the present. The past makes the present seem like it belongs in the past.

14. Our enemies are not terribly smart, but they have their moments of genius. In such moments, they realize that the past is the future, and they twist, rape and exploit the past. Think of Vladimir Putin, who ingeniously revived both the red color of the communist past, and the Tsar's emblematic double-headed eagle to forge an ultra-nationalistic (if somewhat absurd and imbecilic) sense of pride and might. There's a lesson here: upcoming wars happen in the past. Those are the fronts where we barricade our bunker graves.

15. Being dead, past and buried, we vow to use only obsolete media. We shall use cameras, video, software and web tools, but only of the outmoded sort.

16. We shall use all media, we shall perform and make films. As behooves corpses, we shall be fecund. Nothing produces as much as a corpse. But our modes of choice shall be geriatric and senile, and our medium of choice, without a doubt, shall be painting, that astonishing zombie who would not lie down.

The Buried Alive Manifesto

17. There is no meaning. Everything is senseless chaos. Yet this senseless chaos is the hotbed for evil intentions and conspirations. Paranoia is justified.

18. Within the futile muddle of life, there is magic, yet it only occurs under self-contradictory conditions; this can be perceived as the safety valve of magic against those who would aim to exploit it. The first kind of magic is that which occurs only against the will of the magician. The second kind of magic appears at will, even though rarely and through great effort: it is pointless magic. It can serve no aim, but attaining it leaves the magician exhausted. The third kind of magic happens unexpectedly, and only when good-hearted people use it for evil purposes. We are good, and we shall strive to use all three kinds of magic in art.

19. We are friendly, but with friends like us, you don't need enemies. We laugh, and with our laughter you don't need tears.

20. Usually, you cannot see us, and that is our strength. When you do notice us, we appear weak, and that is our strength.

21. We are the Living Dead. When we pass near you, regular folks who believe they are alive, you, who forge yourselves as landlords, when we brush against you we seem almost invisible, hardly a nuisance. Yet you feel a slight chill creeping up your spine. In sensing our presence, something in you discovers for a brief spell that you are like us: displaced, irrelevant, lost, and already dead. Being that we are dead alive, we are a chilly reminder that you are like us, alive but dead.

22. We are the alien hidden inside who sucks your blood like a mosquito while you are sleeping, and like a mouse that makes your house its own. When you wake up, if you ever do, it will be too late. Either you have already become us, or we were long gone, seeking other hosts to exploit. You shall then realize that we were you, and that you are lost.

---

1 The Oberiu Group was a literary avant-garde circle that produced exhilarating and horrifying absurd texts, which was suppressed and persecuted under Stalin. Its members, Daniil Kharms, Alexander Vvdensky and Nikolai Zobolotsky, were forced to write in secrecy, and their production was published only decades after they perished. The Moscow unofficial artists, such as Ilya Kabakov, Victor Pivovarov and others, not recognized as artists in the USSR of the 1960s–'80s, created a closed and secret artistic scene in which they were their own audience, critics, gallerists and historians.

A Complete History of Russia in Jokes
(Incomplete)

by Maxim Komar-Myshkin

During the difficult days of 1991, when food was scarce in Moscow, Maxim and Efim sat down to have dinner.

Maxim said: “Brother, we stood in line for hours, we worked hard to cook the meal, and I know you are very hungry. But may I say a prayer before we start?”

Efim said: “Please do, brother, for I have religious sentiments as well.”

Maxim said: “Oh Lord, bless this food, and also, please make Efim suffer terrible stomach aches later. Amen.”

Efim said: “Brother, may I say my blessing as well? Oh Lord, we thank you for this plentiful meal, and also, Lord, please send Maxim to hell, to suffer eternal damnation. Amen.”

And so it was.

1944 – The War with Germany

Operation Barbarossa was coming to its grim end. The German army was suffering from the horrendous Russian winter. Lieutenant Bohm had survived through much, against all odds. He had witnessed horrors. Most of his comrades had perished. That he had survived so long, devoutly writing monthly letters to his fiancée in Düsseldorf, was miraculous. But no longer. Now, lying in a pool of his own blood, writhing in agony, he was staring at his disemboweled intestines as they quickly started to freeze. The Russian winter would do this to you. The Russian winter killed millions, many of them during those very days. There is a joke in this, something funny to ease all the horror, but I cannot recall it.

Efim was a righteous Jewish doctor. He was the favored doctor of the most important party members, but he was never arrogant; in his spare time he secretly treated the poor for free. Not only that, in his spare time he was also a rabbi and a cantor.

In April 1936, upon Stalin's order, Efim was sentenced to death. As he faced the firing squad, he cried out: "Oh, Lord, I have never asked for anything, but at this moment, for the sake of my beloved wife, who will surely be sent to a labor camp, and for the sake of my three daughters, who will surely be sent to an orphanage and suffer the horrendous disgrace our country bestows upon the children of the condemned, hunger and perhaps also rape and death – for them, dear Lord, I beg for a miracle!"

And lo and behold – a miracle occurred: at that very instant an elephant with two trunks was born in Senegal.[1]

1924 – The Russian Soul

Three distinguished Russians were arguing which of them best represented the passionate Russian soul.

Said the poet Yesenin: "Three nights ago, I got drunk, engaged in a terrible brawl, and lay bleeding in my own vomit. Then, hardly able to move, I burst into tears and wrote a poetic letter to my mama."

Said the author Gorky: "That's nothing. I was so drunk that I mistook your vomit for my mama, burst into tears and desperately tried to hug your vomit."

Said the Cheka chief Dzerzhinsky: "That's nothing: when I saw how Yesenin's vomit was pretending to be Gorky's mother, I pulled out my gun and shot the vomit as a saboteur."

On the morning of June 30th, 1908, eyewitnesses reported a gigantic fireball above the Siberian Tunguska, and an explosion could be heard more than 1,000 kilometers away. The speculation was that this was a meteorite whose impact was tremendously devastating, but the inaccessibility of the area, as well as the troubled political situation at the time, rendered any expedition to the site impossible. In light of that, the Russian government announced it would give an award to the explorer or the scientist who dared attempt the most bold, courageous and difficult expedition.

Most of the proposals did, in fact, offer fanciful ways to arrive at Tunguska against all odds. But in the end, they were obliged to give the award to Professor Myshka Komarov, who offered to invent a time-machine, travel throughout history, and discover for the first time a great Russian philosopher.[2]

1764 – Tsarina Catherine's Affair with Stanislaw Poniatowski

For a number of years Catherine the Great lusted after the handsome Stanislaw Poniatowski, but then, she had enough of him.

"What shall I do, Grigory?" she asked Potemkin.

"I don't see the problem," answered Potemkin. "Make him a gift of 50,000 serfs and a nice plot of land."

"Not with this one," said Catherine. "He believes I am the love of his life, and has audacious ambitions to marry me. There lies the catch: I would like to make him a generous gift, like all dismissed lovers deserve, but at the same time he has to be deeply humiliated."

"You want humiliation through conferring? That's easy," exclaimed Potemkin. "Make him the king of Poland!"[3]

For 200 years the Russians were subjugated to the Tatars until finally, by the end of the 15th century, the Mongol yoke ended. But unfortunately, the Russian rulers adopted certain cruel judicial practices from the Tatars, such as the custom that when a person would appear before the ruler, he should prostrate himself in front of the throne, and beat his forehead on the floor until he bled.

This inhumane custom was terminated 200 years later by the enlightened reforms of Peter the Great. Ever since then, visitors need not break their heads; Russia will break their heads for them.

During the 1650s, a schism occurred in the church following Patriarch Nikon's reforms. The Old Believers were excommunicated and persecuted. During those dramatic days, five holy men discussed the Russian cross, and in particular, the mystical significance of its diagonal lower beam.

Said Bishop Efim the hunchback: "As Saint Andrew taught, the slanted beam indicates that those standing to the right of Christ will inherit heaven, while those on his left shall descend to hell."

Said Brother Sergei of the Sacred Forked Beard: "You are wise, my friend, but you err. A month ago I had a vision in which Jesus appeared before me and explained that one side of his footrest was slanted so as to help him jump higher at the proper moment, and safely reach the bosom of God the Father in heaven."

Father Nicolai of the Many Miraculous Items said: "You are both wondrously wise, much wiser than me, in fact, but in this case you are both wrong. You see – I also saw Jesus in a true vision, and while he said not a word, I could clearly observe that the left leg of our Lord was longer, and his right leg was shorter. Hence, the footrest had to be slanted to allow Jesus to stand on it while on the crucifix."

Monk Georgii of the Swollen Purple Warts said: "I hate to argue, my friends, and I hold Nicolai of the Many Miraculous Items in the highest regard, but it is well known that he tends to confuse left and right. I also saw Jesus in a vision, and it is true that one of his legs was much longer, but it was his right leg, and not his left. The evil Jewish carpenters built the cross this way to mock our Lord and increase his pain."

Father Ardalion the Healer of Mice said: "My beloved Nicolai and Georgii – it is not that Christ had a longer leg: it only appeared that way to you because you had too much vodka. In fact, Christ ordered the lowest bar of the Russian Cross to be slanted so as to remind us Russians that we are all drunkards."

There was a long, thoughtful silence. Then Bishop Efim spoke again: "Our discussion has bestowed great divine knowledge upon me, and I now realize that our miraculous slanted bar holds not one but manifold meanings, and they do not contradict each other: those to the right of Christ shall inherit heaven; God the Son did improve his divine leap upwards thanks to the slanted footrest; the right leg of Christ was longer and the evil Jewish carpenters intentionally built the footrest so the shorter left leg would dangle in the air, while the longer right one would be painfully cramped, but a miracle occurred during crucifixion: our Lord's left leg grew longer while the right one shrunk proportionately; to top it all – all this was part of the divine scheme meant to remind us Russians, Christ's favorite children, that we are all drunks. Now, brothers, make peace with each other, and let us go and kill an Old Believer."

1569 – Malyuta Skuratov and Metropolitan Philip II

Ivan the Terrible had established his dreaded secret police, the Oprichnina, who were spreading death and terror, and whose members were immune from the law. Yet the courageous Metropolitan Philip II would not bow down with fear. In 1568, Philip even rebuked the Tsar in the cathedral and refused to bless him. Soon after, Ivan had Philip deposed on ludicrous charges of sorcery. He, who was once the Metropolitan of Moscow, was now imprisoned in a tiny cell, fettered in chains, with a heavy collar around his neck.

But not for long. On December 23rd, 1569, one of the most ruthless Oprichniki, Malyuta Skuratov, entered Philip's chamber, had the cumbersome collar removed, and said: "Father, I come with good news and bad news. Which would you like to hear first?"

"The bad news," Philip answered.

Malyuta said: "The Tsar sent me here to kill you."

"And the good news?" asked Philip.

"Oh," said Malyuta, "I was only joking: there is no good news."

And he strangled Philip to death with his bare hands.

1 The joke alludes to different historical moments: first, the Moscow show trials (1938–39), the staged judicial humiliation of "enemies of the States" (including Lenin's former cabinet members) before their execution as part of the great purges; and second, the doctors' plot, Stalin's arrest of mostly Jewish doctors in 1952–53, accusing them of attempts to poison Soviet leaders, before Stalin's death in March 1953 brought forth the dismissal of those fabricated charges and the release of the doctors.

2 The point suggested by the punch line is that there were no "great" Russian philosophers. Max Lomberg claims he heard Komar-Myshkin tell an alternative version of this joke, situated in a different historical moment: "The world had always belittled Russian thought and culture, and in most universities, Russian philosophy is not considered worthy of being taught. Lenin decided this wrong must be corrected and so, in 1922, he sent 200 philosophers and intellectuals on a world cruise to discover the great Russian philosopher." This version refers to what is known as "the philosophers' ship": Lenin compiled a list of 228 unwanted thinkers, and expelled most them by two German ships.

3 Stanislaw Poniatowski did not only become the ruler of Poland, but its last king: the final humiliation he suffered at the hands of Catherine was the partition of Poland, which lost it sovereignty, causing its lands to be divided among Prussia, the Austrian Empire and Russia.

Komar-Myshkin's notebooks reveal that he meant for the Russian contempt and aggression towards Poland, and the base nationalism it reveals, to become a leitmotif throughout the jokes chronicle. Some of those jokes where supposed to have the very mention of Poland appear as if it were innately funny, "Poland" serving as a trope for the ridiculously weak and lowly, while other jokes were to employ crucial historical scenes. One of those jokes might have referred to yet another, unrealized division of Poland: the non-aggression Molotov-Ribbentrop pact, signed between Nazi Germany and Stalin's Soviet Union on August 23rd, 1939. The pact included a secret section in which the two nations divided between them the territories of Poland, as well as those of Lithuania, Latvia, Romania, Estonia and Finland. Another joke was to be set in the summer of 1944, when the Polish resistance movement staged its uprising in Warsaw, trusting that they would be supported by the victorious Soviet army, which was already approaching the city's suburbs, and was stationed on the east bank of the Vistula River. Throughout this doomed uprising, Stalin refused to interfere as the Nazis first slew tens of thousands and then, as a punitive measure, destroyed the city and deported its citizens.

An exceedingly cruel joke – even by Komar-Myshkin's standards – was to be set much earlier, in November 1612. In those times of strife, the Polish army managed to capture Moscow. Two Russian leaders, Prince Pozharsky and the merchant Kuzma Minin, managed to outmaneuver the Poles and trap them inside the Kremlin. The exhausted and starving

Poles offered their surrender on the condition of safe passage back to Poland. The Russians promised this safe return, but once the Poles filed out, they were all slain in Red Square. In 2005, Vladimir Putin proclaimed November 4th as a national holiday to commemorate this bloody triumph, which soon became a date celebrated by Russian ultra-nationalists.

The Russian philosopher Nikolai Berdyaev wrote in 1914 about the dispute and the historical animosity between the Russian soul and the Polish soul. He describes this as a true and profound difference, which has to do with Catholic and Orthodox traditions, but also with categorically different character types. Berdyaev, seeing both as types of the Slavic soul, ends with hope: "But these differing souls of peoples are capable not only of understanding and loving each other, but can also sense their belonging to the same ethnic soul conceiving of its Slavic mission to the world" (see: Nikolai Berdyaev, *The Russian and the Polish Soul*, 1914, translated by Fr. S. Janos, http://www.berdyaev.com/berdiaev/berd_lib/1914_178.html). Berdyaev, incidentally, was one of the intellectuals expelled by Lenin on the philosophers' ship in 1922, as mentioned in the preceding footnote.

The *Buried Alive* script adaptation of the Catherine/Poniatowski joke, delivered by Michail Grobman and his wife, Irina Vrubel-Golubkina, is distinctly raunchier than the original version:

Historical Joke Number 2, 1764

[A preliminary shot wanders through the Grobmans' apartment, in a free, jittery fashion, until it arrives at the place where the Grobmans sit. There's a cut, and when the camera is turned on again, it is evidently fixed on a tripod. Seated behind the desk are Ira Vrubel-Golubkina and Michail Grobman. They are flanked by two members of the Buried Alive group, a male on Ira's side (Maxim Komar-Myshkin), and a masked female.

> Ira [snaps at Komar-Myshkin]: Stupid bandit! You think you are a radical artist-terrorist? You are a sissy! Why should the world suffer your bullshit just because you have a tiny penis?

[Komar-Myshkin reaches out to hit her. Cut. Three to four seconds elapse. When the camera is turned on again, Ira's arms and torso are tied tightly, and there are now two guards at her right, the new one being very big and muscular. One of her eyes is conspicuously bruised, and her hair is frazzled. Pause. Grobman looks at the girl at his left, she nods. He looks straight at the camera, waits a few seconds and begins to read.]

> Grobman: My name is Michail Grobman. I am a very important international artist, writer, poet and thinker. I was one of the founding members of the Second Russian Avant-Garde, and when I immigrated to Israel I became the leader of *Leviathan,* one of the most visionary and important groups of artists in the history of the nation. Next to me is my wife, Irina Vrubel-Golubkina. She is one of the foremost women of letters worldwide. She is the chief editor of *Zerkalo,* the most important cultural publication in the Russian language worldwide. A few hours ago we were overpowered by a group of

young members of the Buried Alive group. They have taken over our apartment in Tel Aviv, where we are still being held. Our physical condition is perfect. We were not harmed in any way during our captivity. [Pause.] According to the orders given to us by Buried Alive, we are about to read a historical joke in the form of a dialogue between the Tsarina Ekaterina the Great, who was famous for her incredible sexual appetite ...

[At this point, Ira seeks the attention of the muscular man next to her. He bows down and she whispers a request in his ear. He hesitates for a moment, decides to consent, and pulls out a cigarette. It takes him a moment to realize that he needs to put it in her mouth, being that her hands are tied. He lights it for her. From now on he has to facilitate her smoking. Grobman renews his recitation.]

Grobman: We are about to read a historical joke in the form of a dialogue between the Tsarina Ekaterina the Great, who was famous for her incredible sexual appetite, and the wonderful Potemkin, who was initially her lover, but later, besides being an army leader and a statesman, became her confidant and perhaps the strongest man in the kingdom after the ruler herself. We shall narrate the joke in the form of a dialogue. [Short pause.] I will be Potemkin and Irina will be the Tsarina. For a number of years, Ekaterina the Great fornicated with the handsome Stanislaw Poniatowski, but then she got bored with him, and turned to Potemkin for advice.

Ira: What shall I do, my dear Grigory Potemkin? This Poniatowski was a fair lover, somewhat above average in penis size, and able to hold his own in bed. He also has a very cute ass, and always readily agreed to things others found difficult to swallow. Talking about swallowing, I even had him lick horse sperm from my thigh several times after copulating with my sweet animals. But he is too gentle and weak for me, and by now he quite annoys me.

Grobman: I don't see the problem, my dear Ekaterina the Great. Give him 50,000 serfs as a gift and a nice lot of land, and move on to the next lover. You have always been very kind to the lovers you dismiss.

Ira: It is not simple to be good with this one. Poniatowski believes I am the love of his life, and has audacious ambitions to marry me. There lies the catch: I would like to make him a generous gift, like all dismissed lovers deserve, but at the same time he has to be deeply humiliated, so that he will realize he has no chance with me at all, horse sperm or not. And we are talking about the man who said "thank you" after I had an old castrated negro thrash his buttocks raw, while music was performed by a band of naked balalaika players. And did I mention the horse sperm?

Grobman: Yes, your highness, my sweetheart – you did mention the horse sperm. But back to the paradox: you want a gift that would be kind and humiliating at the same time?

Ira: Exactly. I want a grand gift that would be as offensive as a curse!

Grobman: Then there is one obvious solution: make him the king of Poland!

The Biography of the Object *

by Sergei Tret'iakov

Tret'iakov wrote "The Biography of the Object" (or "The Biography of the Thing" *[biografiia veshchi]*) at a time when the champions of the new proletarian realism were campaigning for the reinstatement of the sovereign human subject at the center of the fictional narrative. Under the slogan of the "living person" *[zhivoi chelovek]*, members of VAPP (The All-Union Association of Proletarian Writers) and the *Na literaturnom postu* [On Literary Guard] group advanced the psychological novel as the most suitable means for constructing an image of the person that was nuanced and complex enough to reflect the psychic density and existential inscrutability of human experience. But as some members of Lef pointed out, this cultivation of psychological complexity usually yielded stories that did not make sense. For example, Osip Brik noted in a review of Fyodor Gladkov's *Cement* (1925) that it was impossible for the reader to reconcile the novel's two plots: the protagonist Gleb's reorganization of production at the local cement factory, and the simultaneous foundering of his relationship with his wife. Although Gleb the producer and Gleb the husband coincide chronologically, they never converge. Brik explained that the schizoid structure of the novel's hero originated in a literary device that compresses multiple actants into a single character. What seemed to endow the heralded "living person" with emotional complexity and richness was, in other words, just an aesthetic convention which in no way corresponded to the actual psychic structure of living people. The hero of the psychological novel was not one person, but a compound figuration of the multitude, as Brik explained: "Heroism is a literary device that makes possible the attribution to a single person (the hero) a sum of deeds (exploits) that in reality have been produced by the labors of an entire series of people." [1]

The Biography of the Object

Tret'iakov's biography of the object can be understood as a method for unpacking these impossibly dense accumulations of deeds within the device of the hero. Unlike the traditional novel, which filtered the complicated interactions of manifold social groups through the impacted psyche of a single character, Tret'iakov's object biography is a kind of anti-Bildungsroman that focused not on psychological consistency, but on people who are declined by a variety of production processes. If the traditional novel was held together by the hero, the biography of the object was held together by the act. The latter thus responded to Brik's call for a literature organized not around the living person, but around the living deed: "We need to give literature the following task: not to provide us with people, but with the deed; not to describe people, but the deed; not to be interested in people, but in deeds. The human being is important to us not because he experiences emotion, but because of his role in the deed." 2

Of course, a new method of storytelling based on the act rather than on psychic interiority would, as Tret'iakov notes in this essay, require completely restructuring the novel's closed narrative economy. This overhaul was not just a matter of enthroning objects at the center of the novel where the hero once was, for that would still leave the disproportionate and latent humanist structure of the novel intact. What was needed was a narrative technics that would not hierarchize the space of representation in this "Ptolemaic" fashion, one which would take the points of intensity concentrated by the novel's intrigue in the hero's emotional biography and distribute them among a plurality of actants over the entire work. The result would be a narrative free of one of the novel's major vices, what Brik elsewhere called tsel'nost' *[unity]: the sense of fatefulness that the novel generates by concatenating all events within the psyche of its hero. In a literature that follows the red thread of the psychological plot, each event follows upon the next in an orderly teleology, a sequence that Tretiakov characterizes here as "fatalist." (Roland Barthes too would describe narrative as "language of Destiny" in* S/Z *[1970].) But in a literature organized around the act, in the biography of the object, each event is succeeded by a potentially infinite number of other events. Its structure is not linear, but isotropic. Only a story constructed in this way, Tretiakov suggests, would make it possible to follow "the development of a large number of people without disrupting the proportions of the narrative." It would be an epic of the collective.*

*

In the classical novel that is based upon the individual hero's biography, the relative scale of the characters is largely reminiscent of Egyptian wall paintings. The colossal pharaoh is on the throne at the center; near him, in a slightly smaller size, is his wife; still smaller are the ministers and army commanders; and finally, in faceless heaps of copper coins, is the entire varied mass of the population: the servants, the soldiers, the slaves.

The hero is what holds the novel's universe together. The whole world is perceived through him. The whole world is, furthermore, essentially just a collection of details that belong to him.

Idealist philosophy asserts that "man is the measure of all things"; "man - how proud that sounds";[3] "when man dies, so too dies the world"; this idealist philosophy is sovereign in the novel's structure. Indeed, these formulas are nothing other than the grains of sand around which bourgeois art crystallizes - the art of an epoch of open rivalry and rapacious competition.

In order to determine the power of this idealism in the novel, you have only to consider the weight within it of the objective world (the world of things and processes) relative to the weight of the subjective world (the world of emotions and experiences).

The Onegins, Rudins, Karamazovs, and Bezukhovs are the suns of independent planetary systems around which characters, ideas, objects, and historical processes orbit submissively. More accurately, they aren't even suns, but just common planets that have mistaken themselves for suns and have not yet come into contact with a Copernicus who will put them in their place. When today's obedient students of idealist literature try to "reflect reality synthetically" by constructing literary systems with Samgins, Virineias, and Chumalovs at their center, they end up recreating the same ancient Ptolemaic system of literature.

In the novel, the leading hero devours and subjectivizes all reality. The art of different periods shows the individual from different perspectives. More precisely, it shows his integration into a variety of systems. These systems can be economic, political, productive-technical, everyday, biological, or psychological.

The classical novelist is not interested in the person as a participant in an economic process. Do not forget that idealist art has its roots in feudalism, where the dominant figure is that of an idle, magisterial, and privileged rentier. Isn't this the origin of the novel's contempt for the laboring person? Do you see how little space is accorded to the hero's technical and productive specialization. Heroic engineers, doctors, and financiers do exist in the novel, but typically only a minimal number of lines are given to what they do and how they do it. But then again, the novel has a lot to say about how they kiss, how they eat, how they enjoy themselves, how they languish, and how they die.

Because the novel's characters have been removed from the systems of production and transposed into the psychological systems of the everyday, the novel usually takes place in the hero's leisure time. This produces particularly monstrous results in contemporary novels by "students of the classics" who write of the "suffering of proletarian Werthers in their leisure hours."

The classical novel, which barely even touched upon the active person in his professional life, was similarly unwilling to analyze him within political, social, or physiological systems. If we recall that the novel's aesthetic rules invented a particular fantastic illness for the hero and the heroine - the nervous fever - and that it also made sure that wounds and grave illnesses never afflicted the hero below the belt, we come to realize just how arbitrary the novel's physiology actually is.

With its doctrines of predetermination and doom, with its absolute dominance of elementary forces, idealist philosophy had its way with the novel, which began to interpret the human from a fatalist perspective. The novel cultivated genetic psychophysiological traits rather than the professional diseases characteristic of social groups. Recall all the tragedies of the epileptics, the freaks, the sick, the insane, and the cripples. The novel was interested only in unconditioned reflexes. Hence the tragedies of hunger, love, and jealousy "as such."

Sociopolitical conflicts were conceived only as breaches of ethics (betrayal and treason) and in terms of the nervous disorders that arose from them (the pangs of conscience). Following this course, the person became completely irrational within the novel. Pathological emotional hypertrophy removed him from social and intellectual systems. Where else but in the novel can emotions celebrate such an absolute and insolent victory over the intellect, over knowledge, over technical and organizational experience?

In a word: the novel based upon the human hero's biography is fundamentally flawed and, currently, the best method for smuggling in the contraband of idealism.

This applies even to those attempts to incorporate the hero using different methods, which approach him from a professional, social, and physiological perspective. The power of the novel's canon is so great that every professional moment is perceived as an annoying digression from the novel's usual plot, and every piece of physiological information is regarded either as a symptom of a psychological experience or a tedious diversion of the reader's attention.

I came up against this in my own practice when I wrote the bio-interview *Den Shi-khua,* the biography of a real person whom I followed with the highest possible degree of objectivity. The reader is constantly tempted to lapse into the habitual routines of biographical psychologism, and the factual numbers and observations are on the threshold of aesthetic metaphor and hyperbole.

Despite the fact that a substantial number of objects and production processes have been incorporated into the narrative, the figure of the hero is distended. Thus, this figure, instead of being conditioned by these objects and influences, begins to condition them himself.

The biography of the object is an expedient method for narrative construction that fights against the idealism of the novel. It is extremely useful as a cold shower for littérateurs, a superb means for transforming the writer - that eternal "anatomist of chaos" and "tamer of the elements" - into someone at least somewhat educated about the present. And most important, the biography of the object is useful because it puts the novel's distended character in his place.

The compositional structure of the "biography of the object" is a conveyer belt along which a unit of raw material is moved and transformed into a useful product through human effort. (This is how Pierre Hamp constructs his works, in particular his *Svezhaia Ryba* [Fresh Fish].)

The biography of the object has an extraordinary capacity to incorporate human material. People approach the object at a cross-section of the conveyer belt. Every segment introduces a new group of people. Quantitatively, it can track the development of a large number of people without disrupting the narrative's proportions. They come into contact with the object through their social aspects and production skills. The moment of consumption occupies only the final part of the entire conveyer belt. People's individual and distinctive characteristics are no longer relevant here. The tics and epilepsies of the individual go unperceived. Instead, social neuroses and the professional diseases of a given group are foregrounded.

While it takes considerable violence to force the reader of a biographical novel to perceive some quality of the hero as social, in the "biography of the object" the opposite is the case: here the reader would have to force himself to imagine a given phenomenon as a feature of a character's individual personality.

In the "biography of the object" emotion finds its proper place and is not felt as a private experience. Here we learn the social significance of an emotion by considering its effect on the object being made.

Remember too that the conveyer belt moving the object along has people on *both* sides. This longitudinal section of the human masses is one that cuts across classes. Encounters between employers and workers are not catastrophic, but organic moments of contact. In the biography of the object we can view class struggle synoptically at all stages of the production process. There is no reason to transpose class struggle onto the psychology of the individual by erecting a special barricade that he can run up to waving a red banner.

On the object's conveyer belt, the revolution is heard as more resolute, more convincing, and as a mass phenomenon. For the masses necessarily share in the biography of the object.

Thus: not the individual person moving through a system of objects, but the object proceeding through the system of people - for literature this is the methodological device that seems to us more progressive than those of classical belles lettres.

We urgently need books about our economic resources, about objects made by people, and about people that make objects. Our politics grow out of economics, and there is not a single second in a person's day uninvolved in economics or politics. Books such as *The Forest*, *Bread*, *Coal*, *Iron*, *Flax*, *Cotton*, *Paper*, *The Locomotive*, and *The Factory* have not been written. We need them, and it is only through the "biography of the object" that they can be adequately realized.

Furthermore, once we run a human along the narrative conveyer belt like an object, he will appear before us in a new light and in his full worth. But that can happen only after we have reoriented the reception practices of readers raised on belles lettres toward a literature structured according to the method of the "biography of the object."

1 “Biografiia veshchi,” in *Literatura Fakta,* ed. Nikolai Chuzhak (Moscow: Federatsiia, 1929), 66–70.

2 Osip Brik, “Pochemu ponravilsia Tsement,” in Chuzhak, *Literatura Fakta,* 85.

3 Osip Brik, “Razgrom Fadeeva,” in Chuzhak, *Literatura Fakta,* 93.

4 Reference to Maksim Gorky’s *The Lower Depths.* See “Art in the Revolution and the Revolution in Art,” 13, note 4.

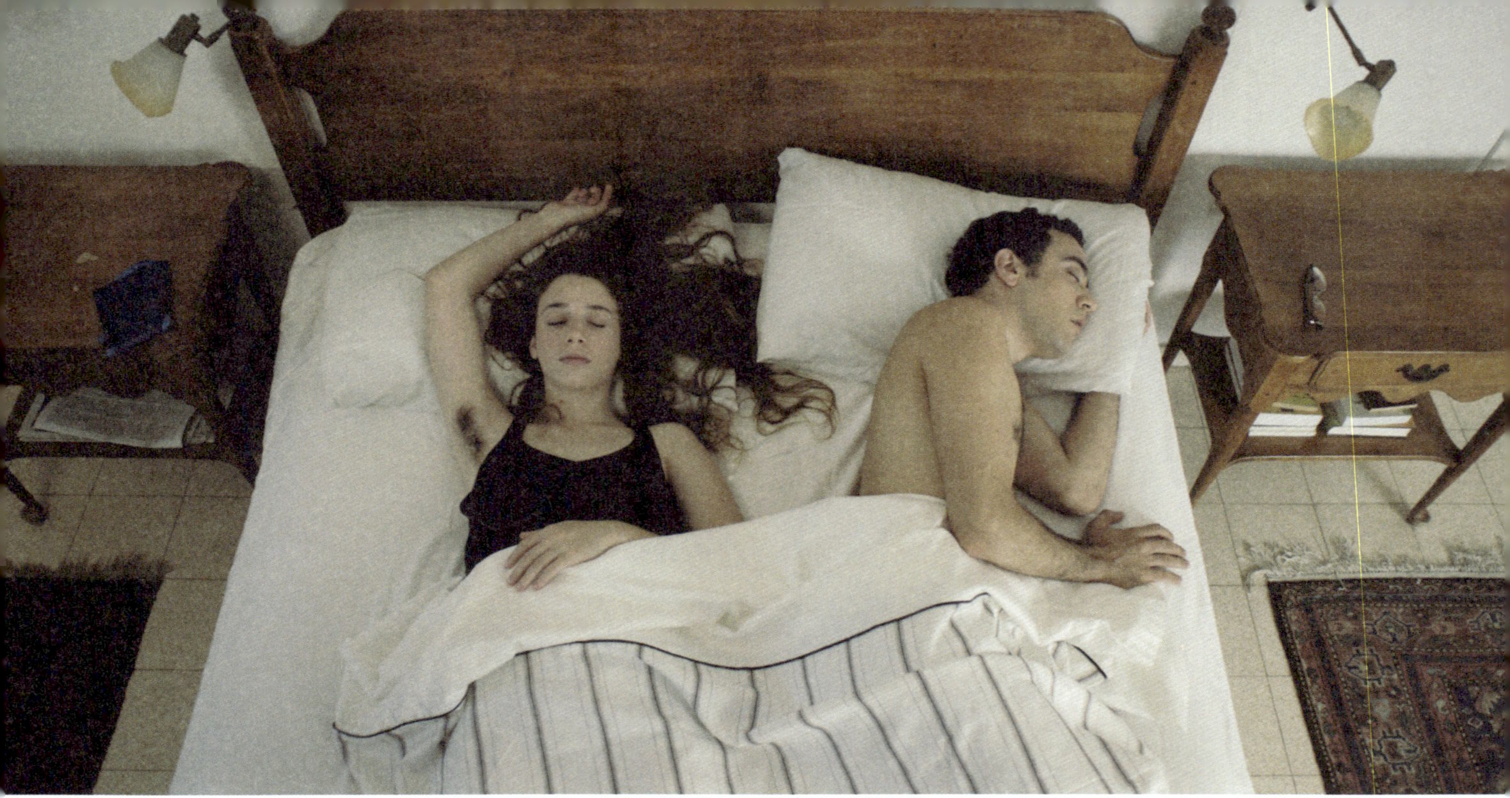

116–117

The Dust Channel, 2016. Video stills

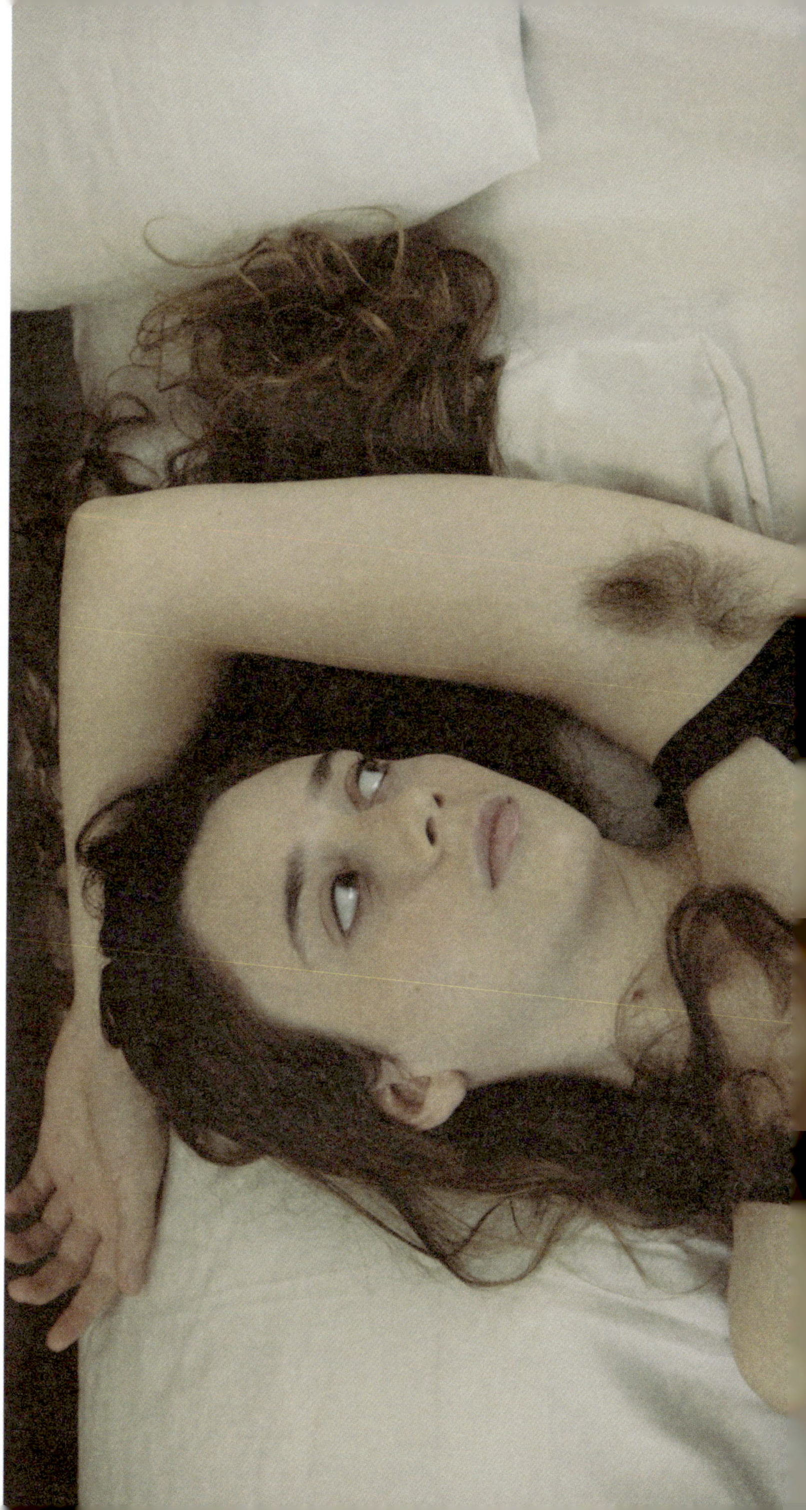

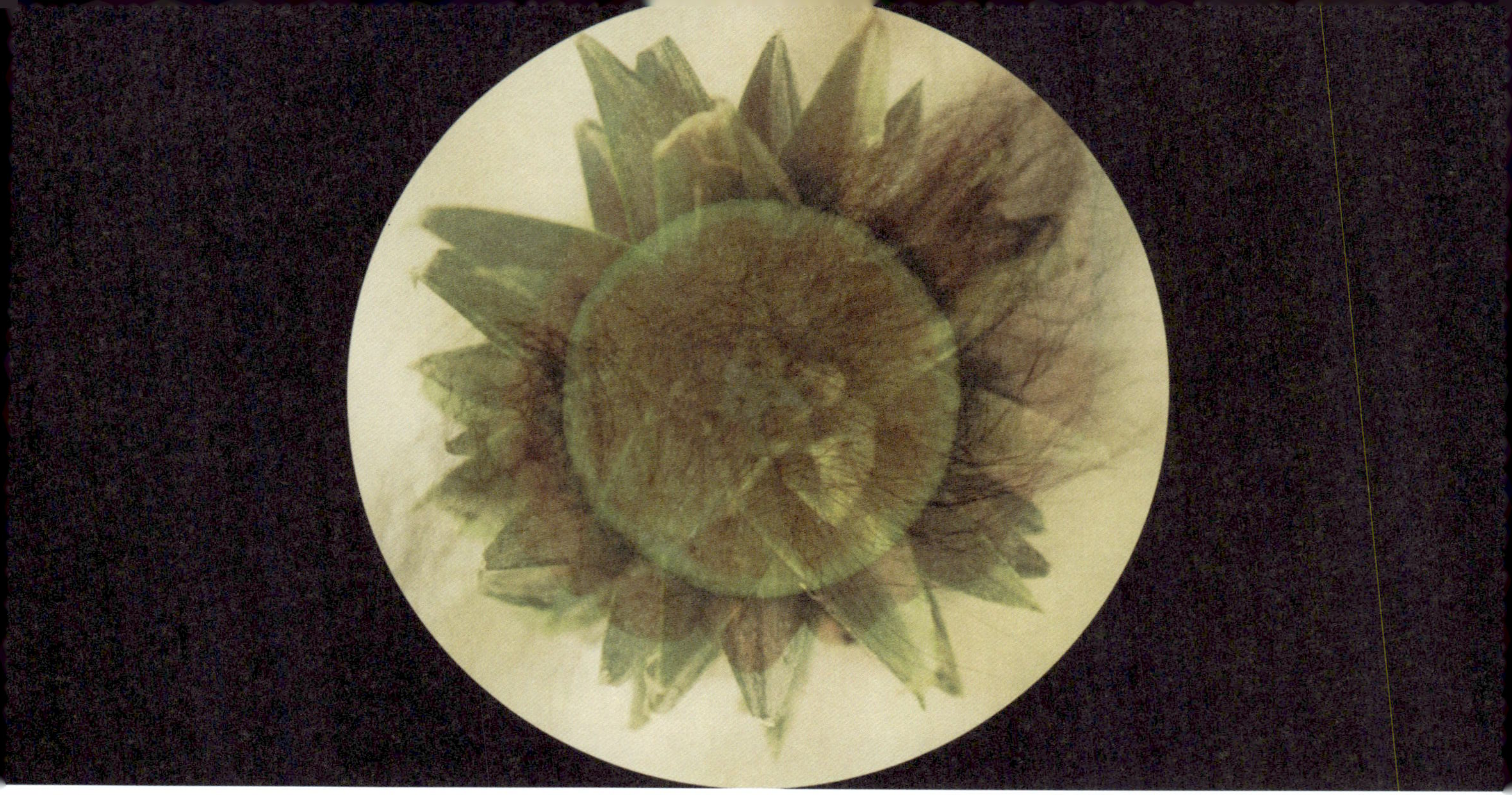

118 – 119 *The Dust Channel*, 2016. Video stills

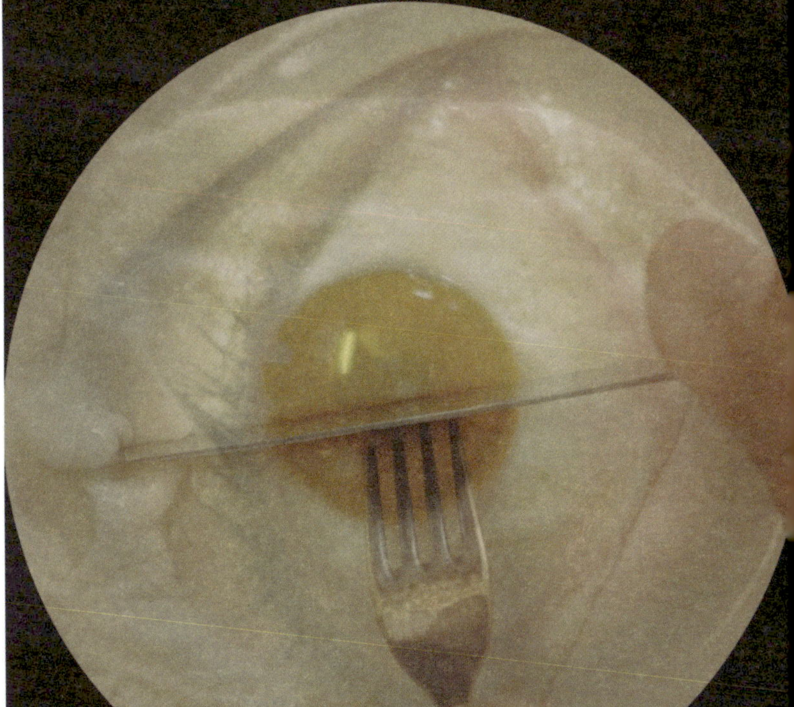

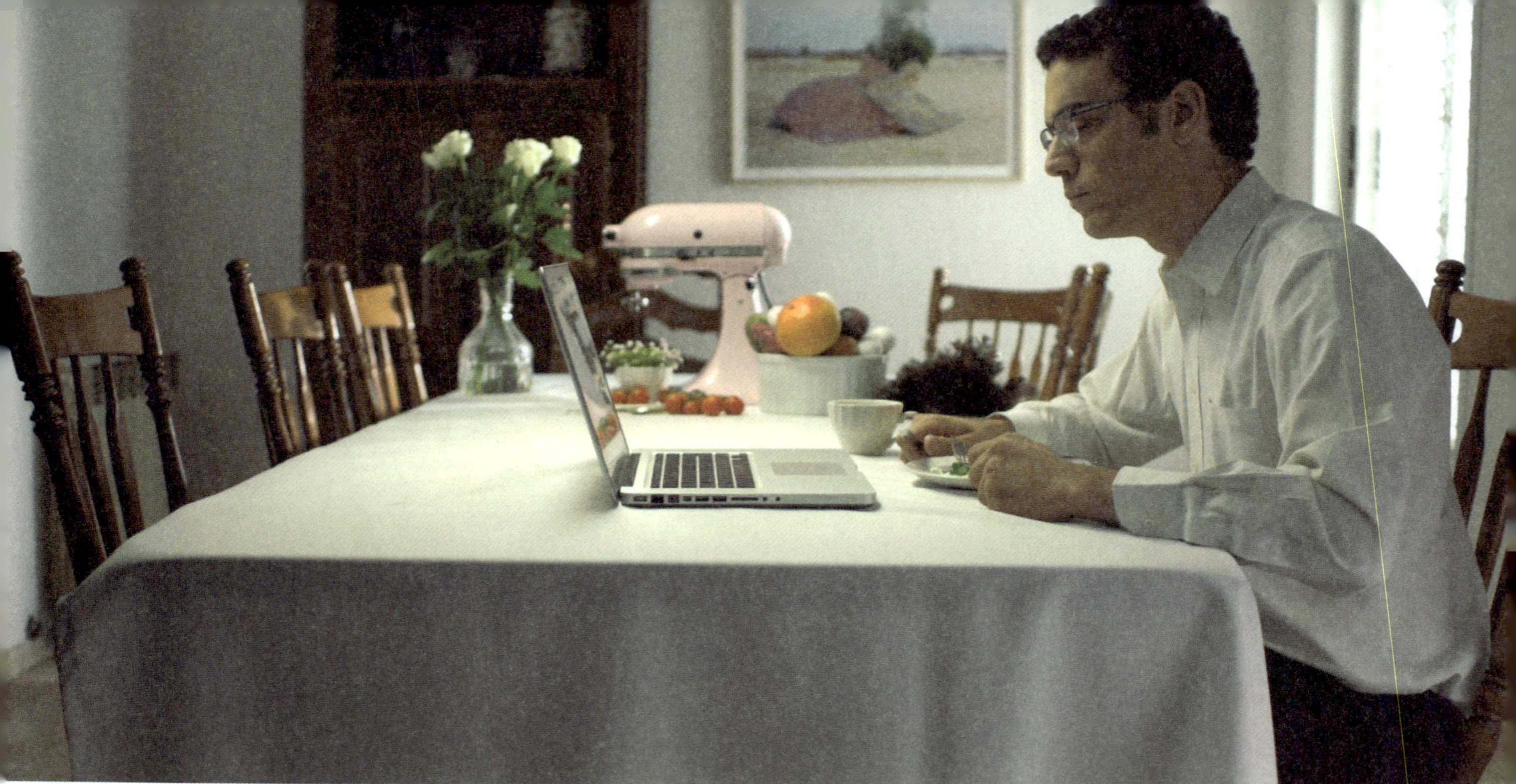

120 – 121

The Dust Channel, 2016. Video stills

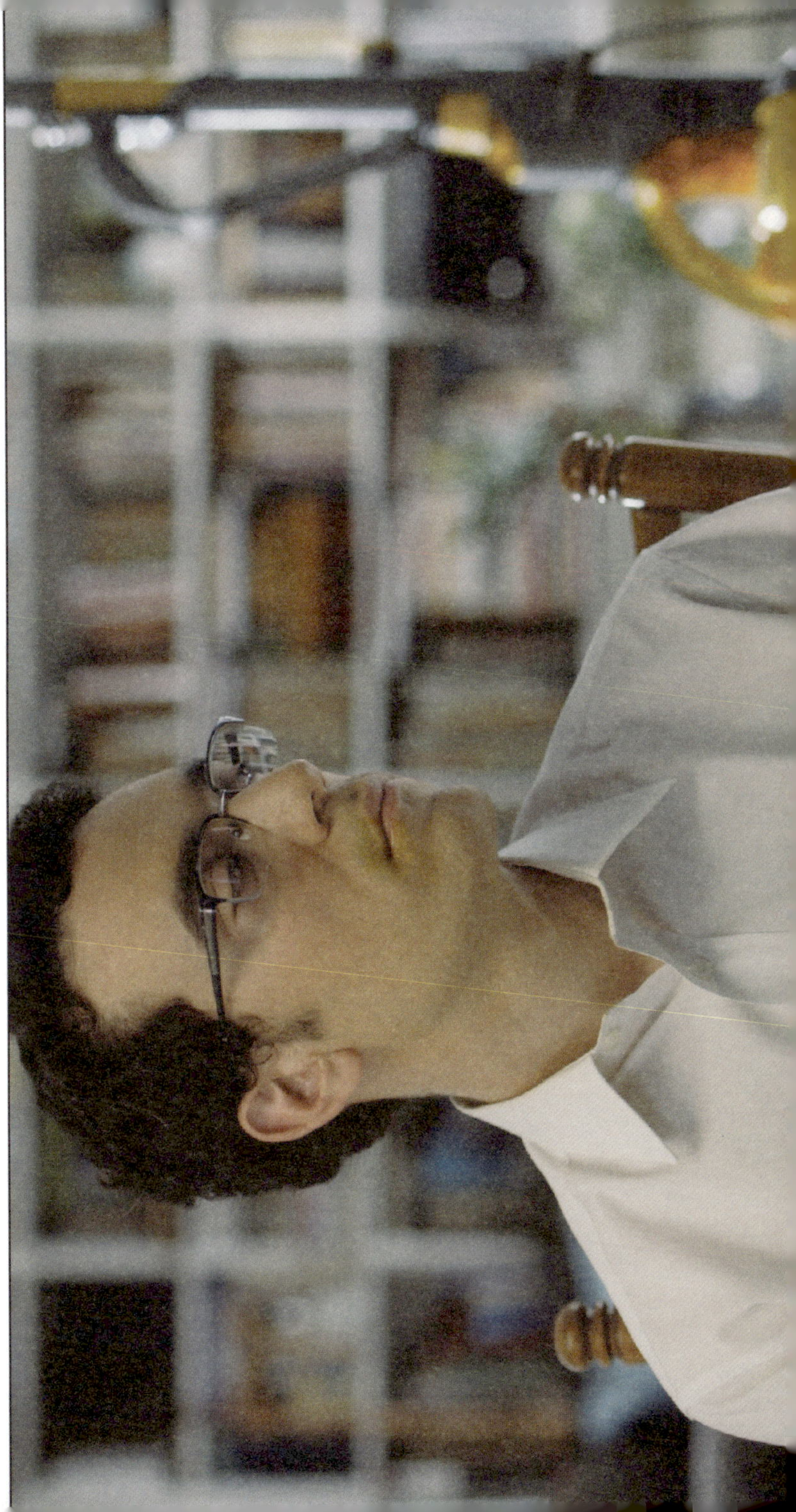

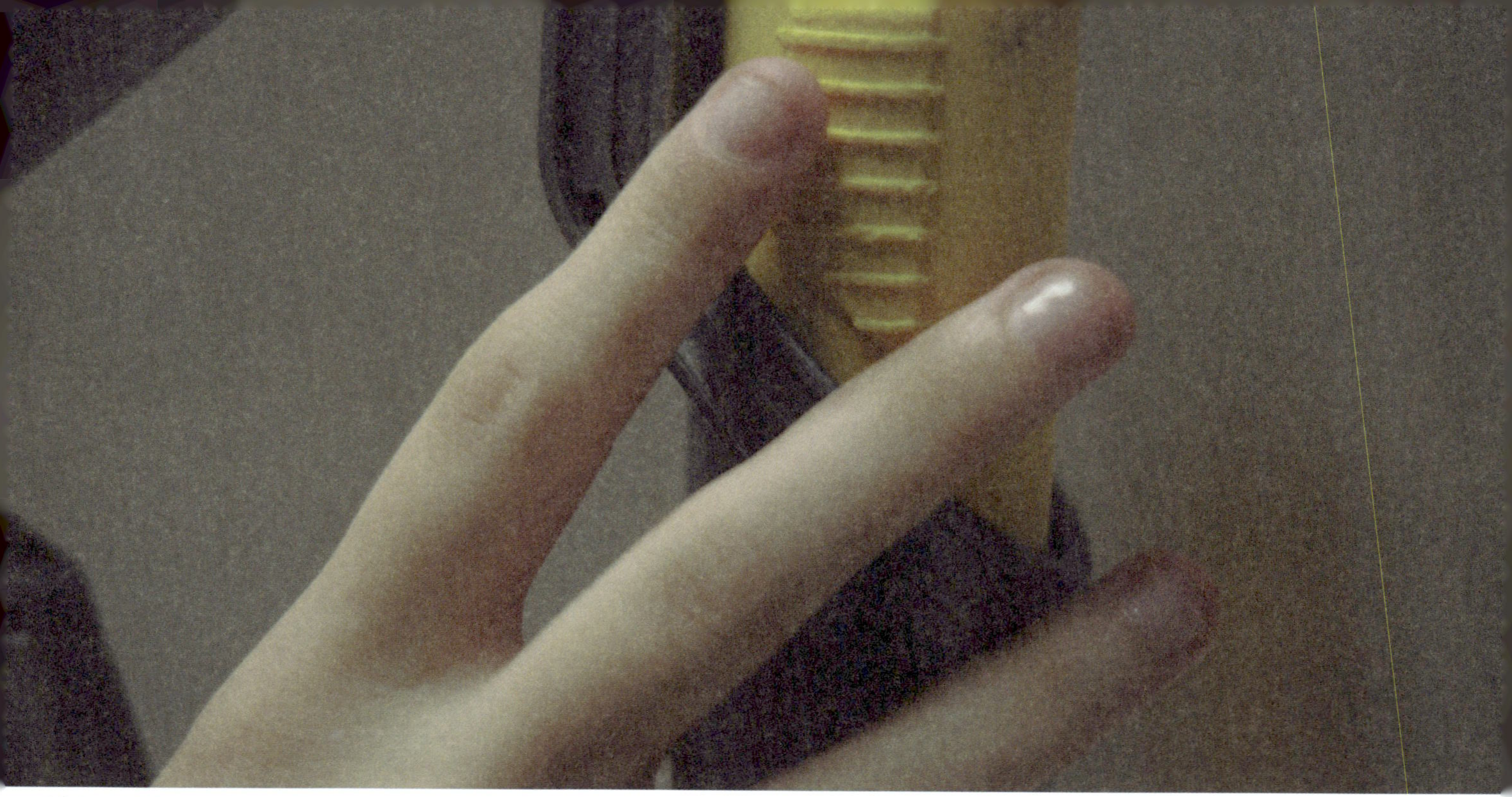

122 – 123 *The Dust Channel*, 2016. Video stills

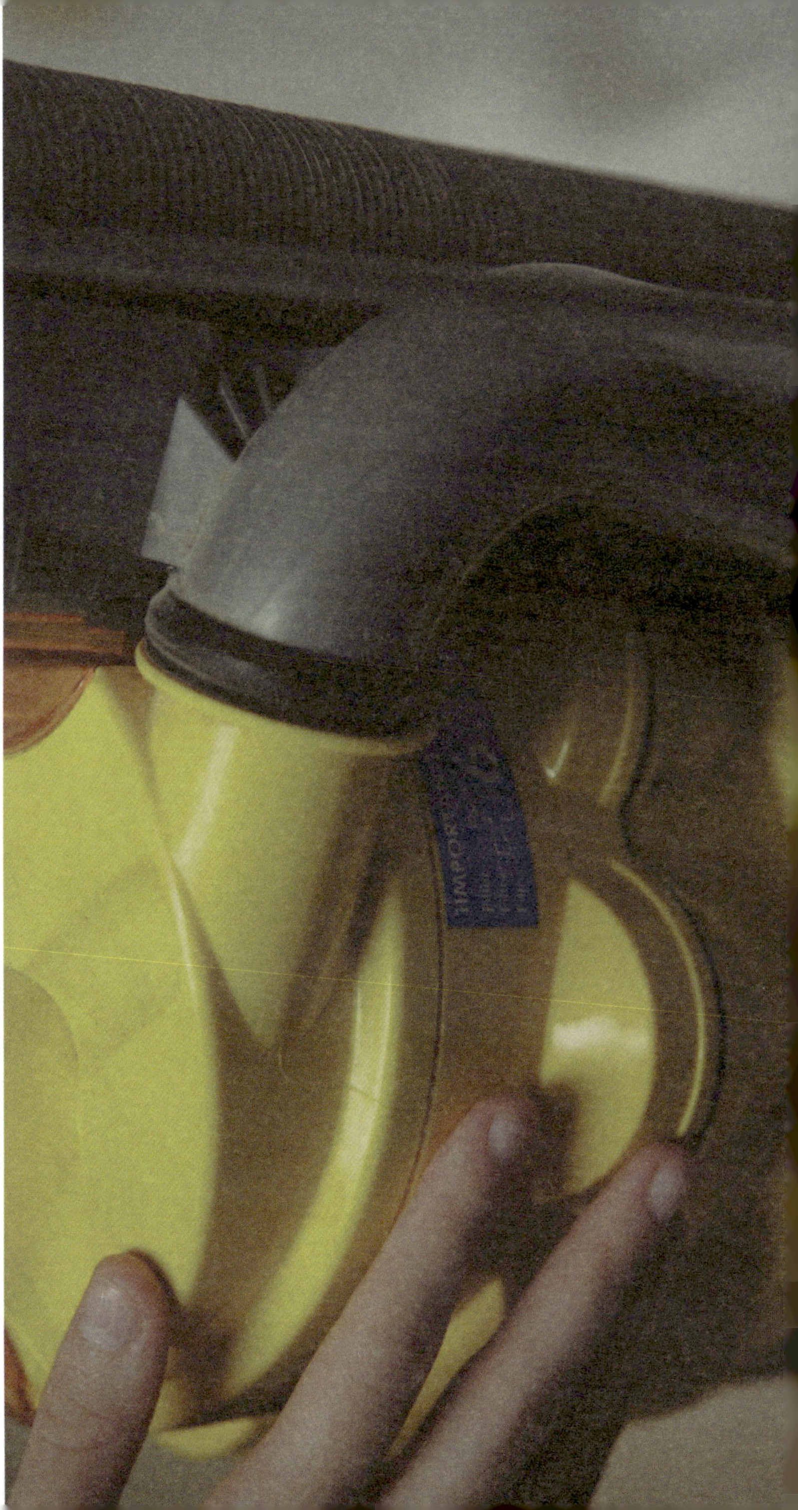

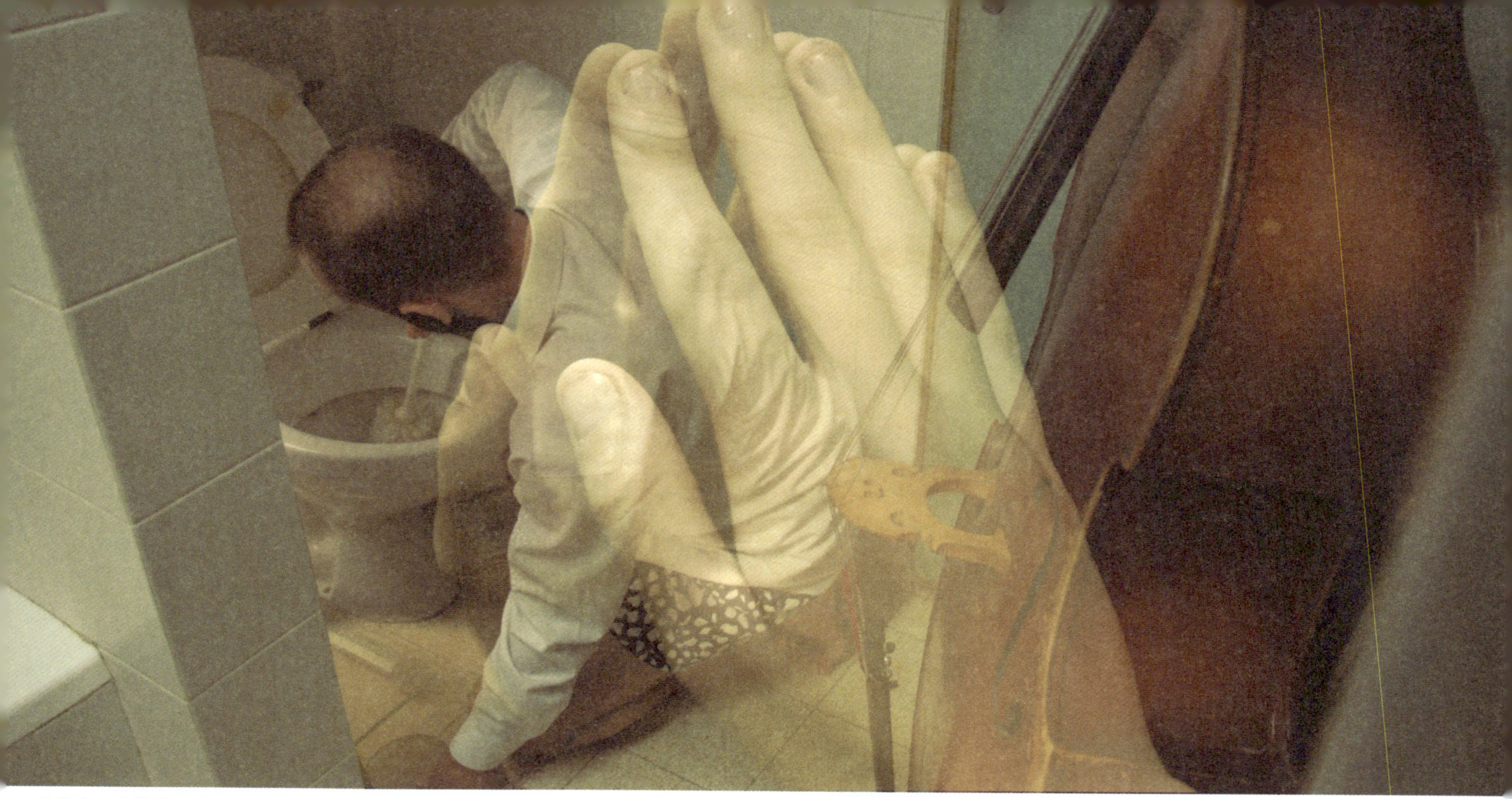

124 – 125

The Dust Channel, 2016. Video stills

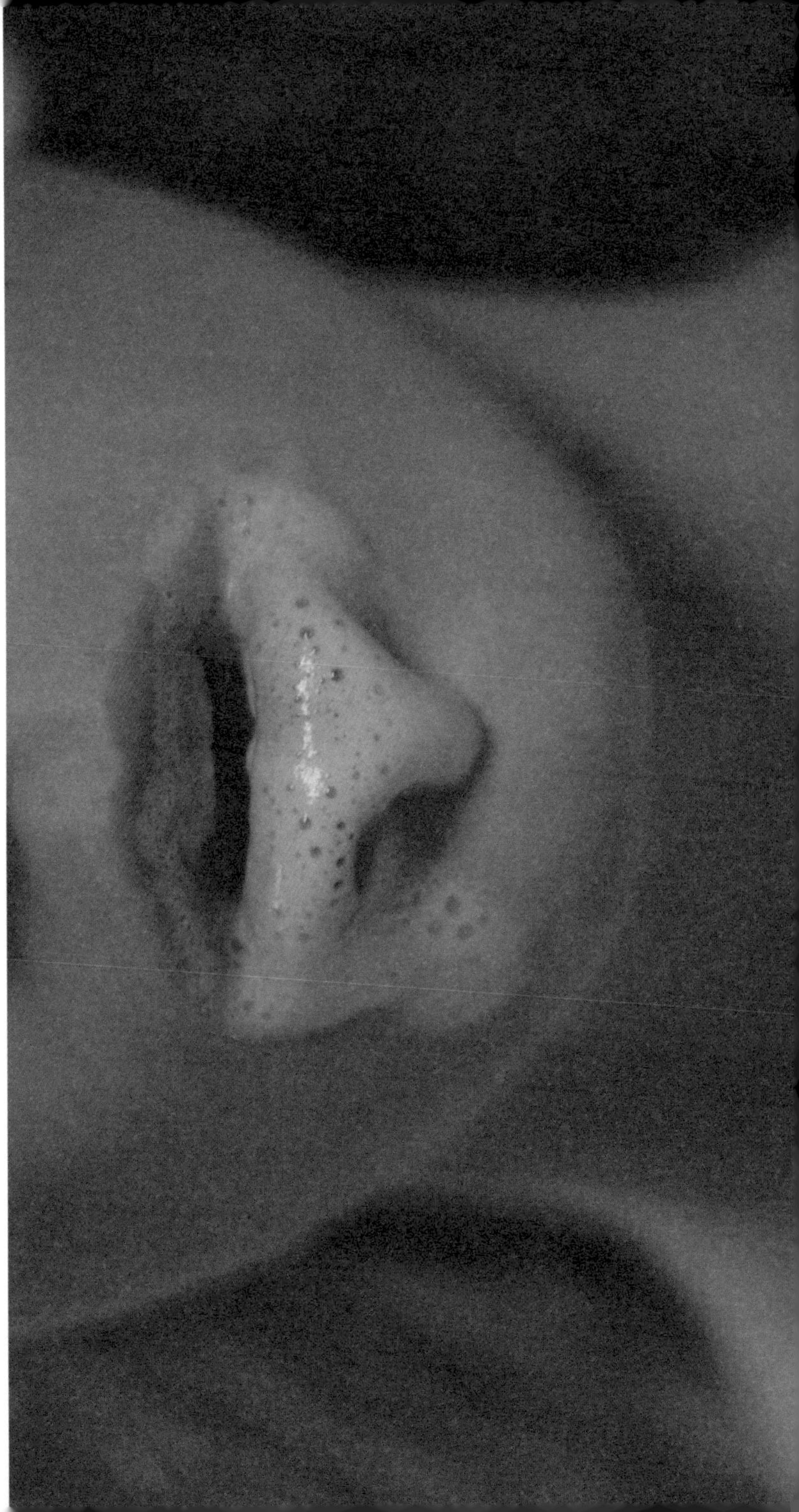

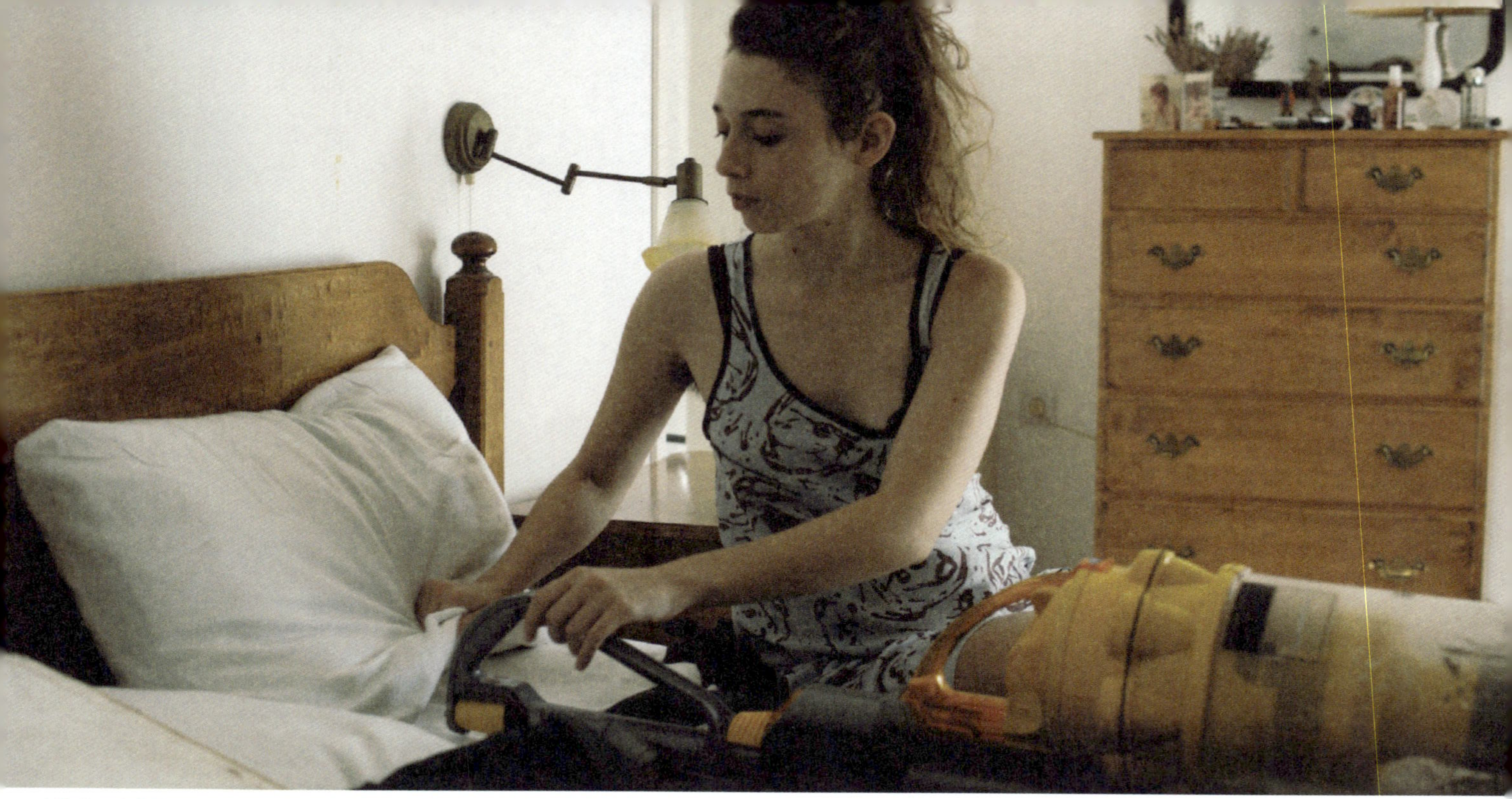

126 – 127

The Dust Channel, 2016. Video stills

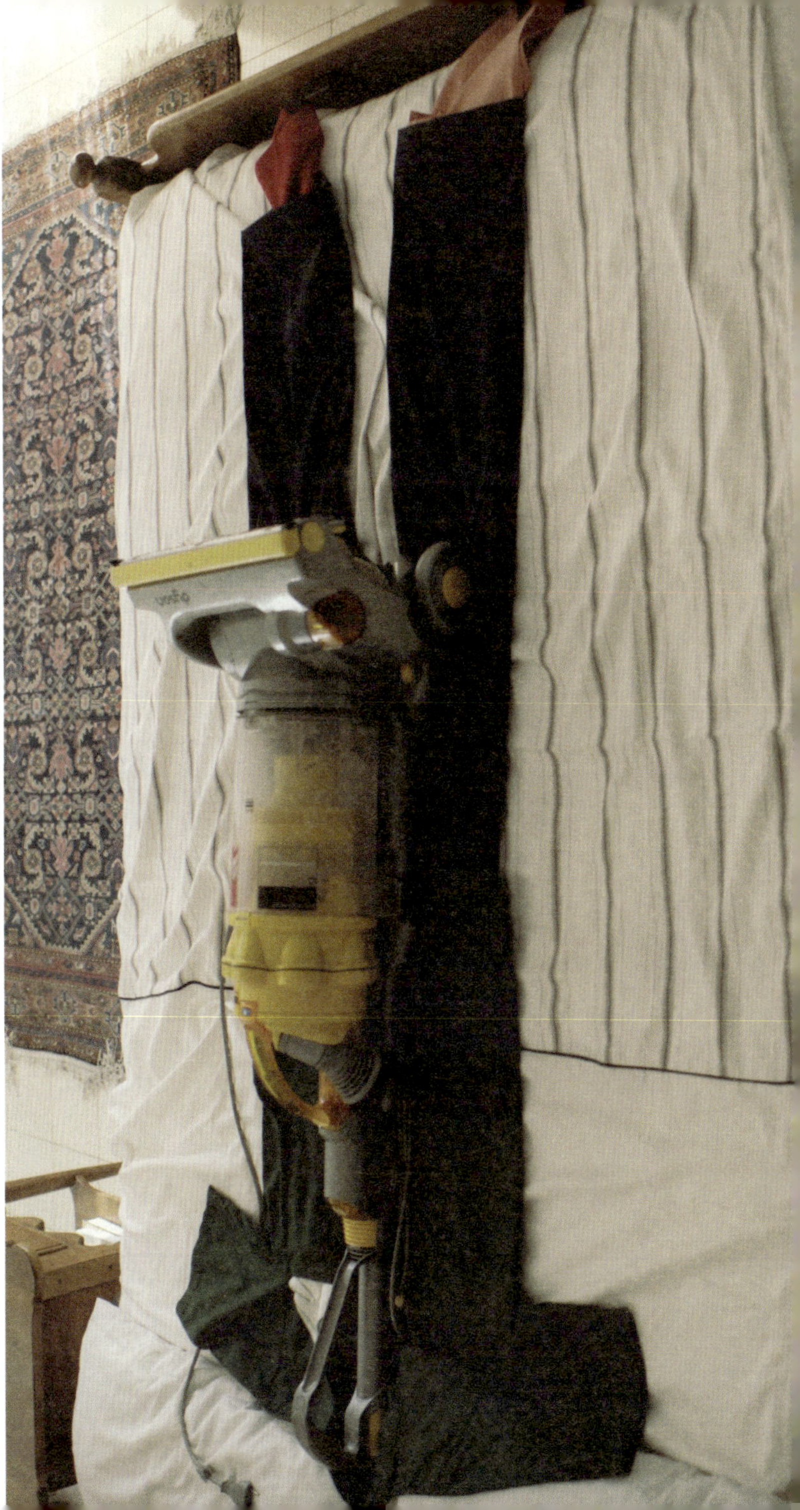

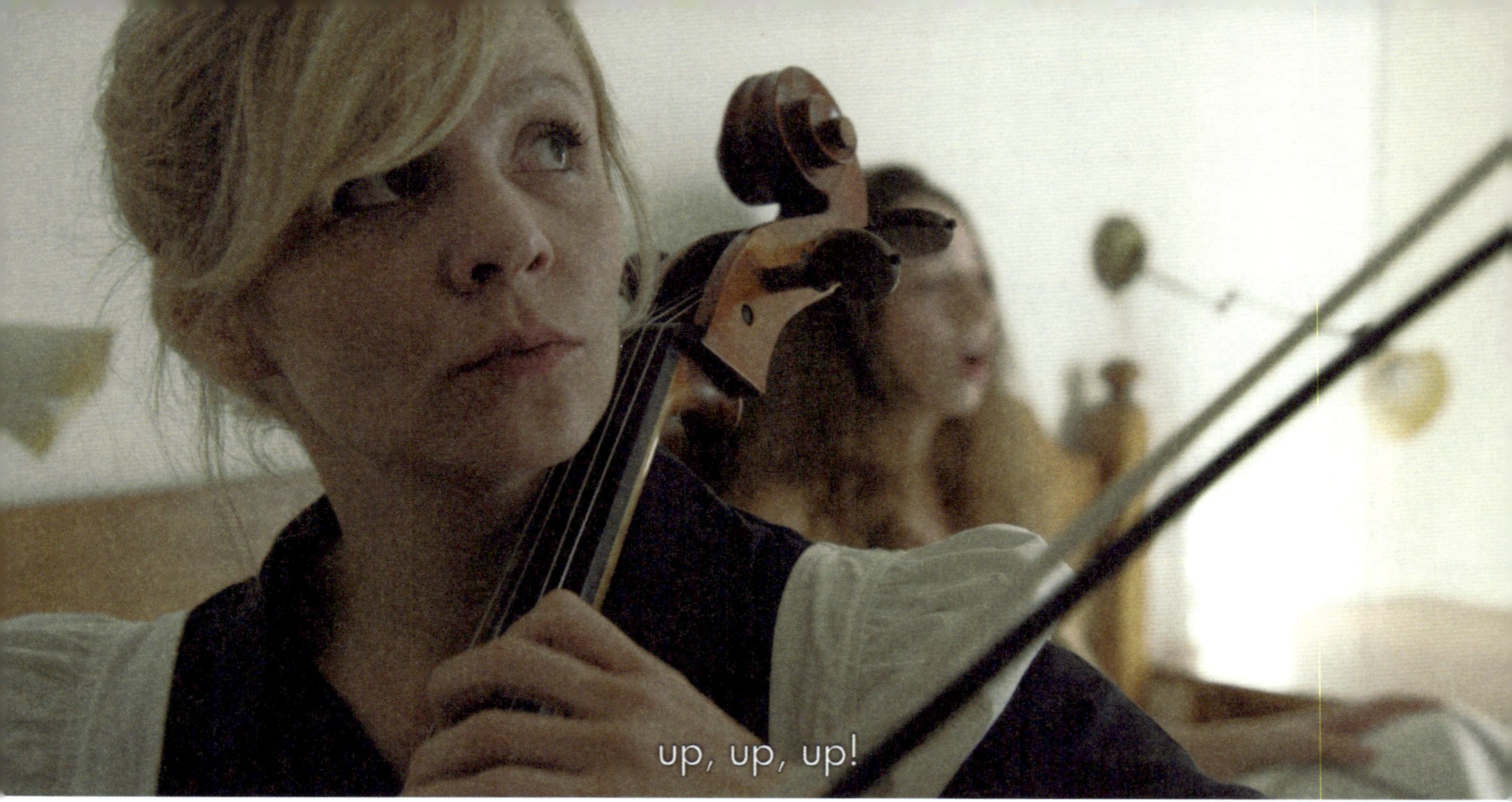

128 – 129 *The Dust Channel*, 2016. Video stills

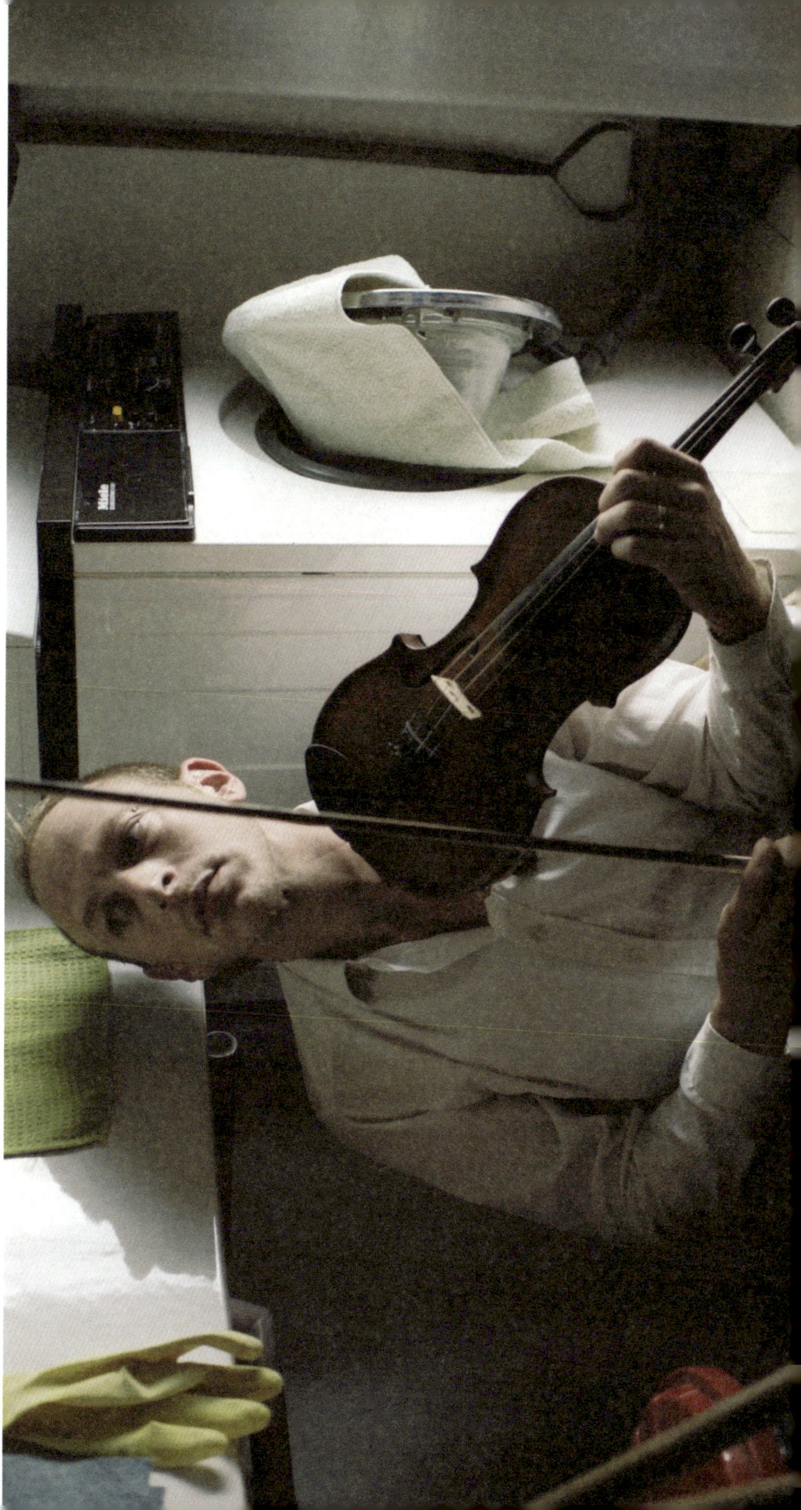
Miele

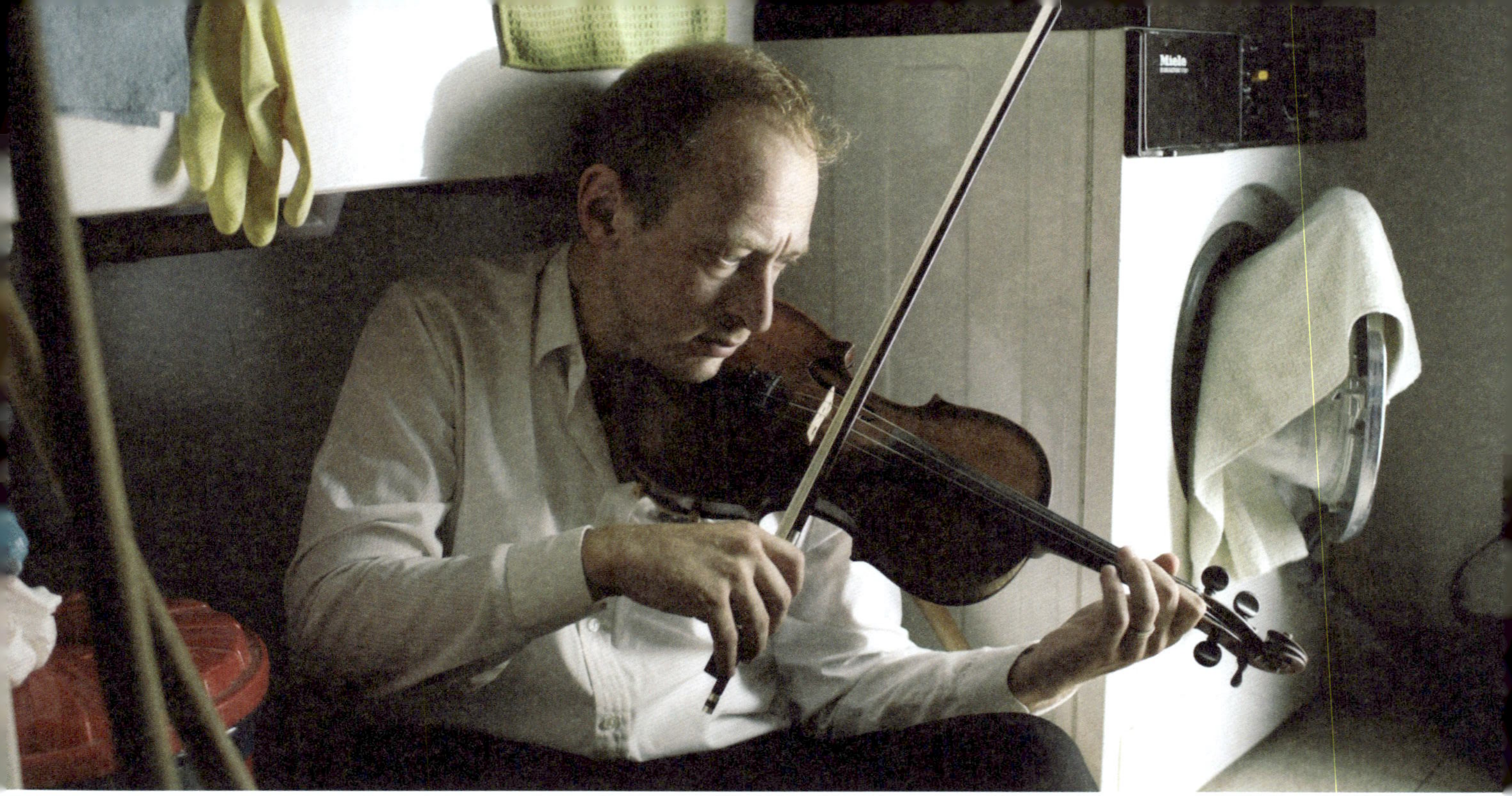

130 – 131 *The Dust Channel*, 2016. Video stills

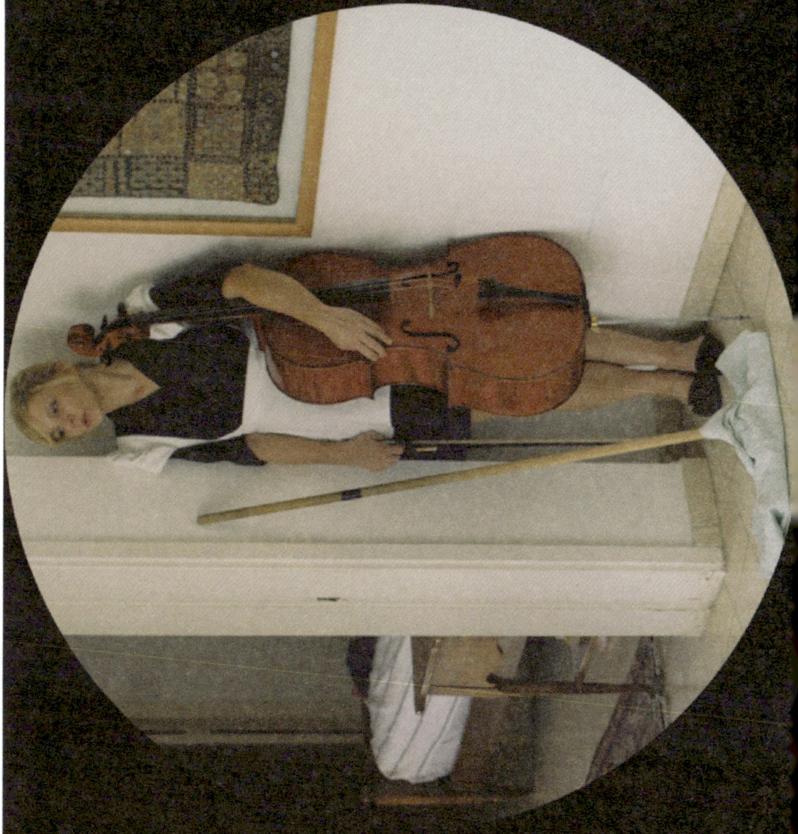

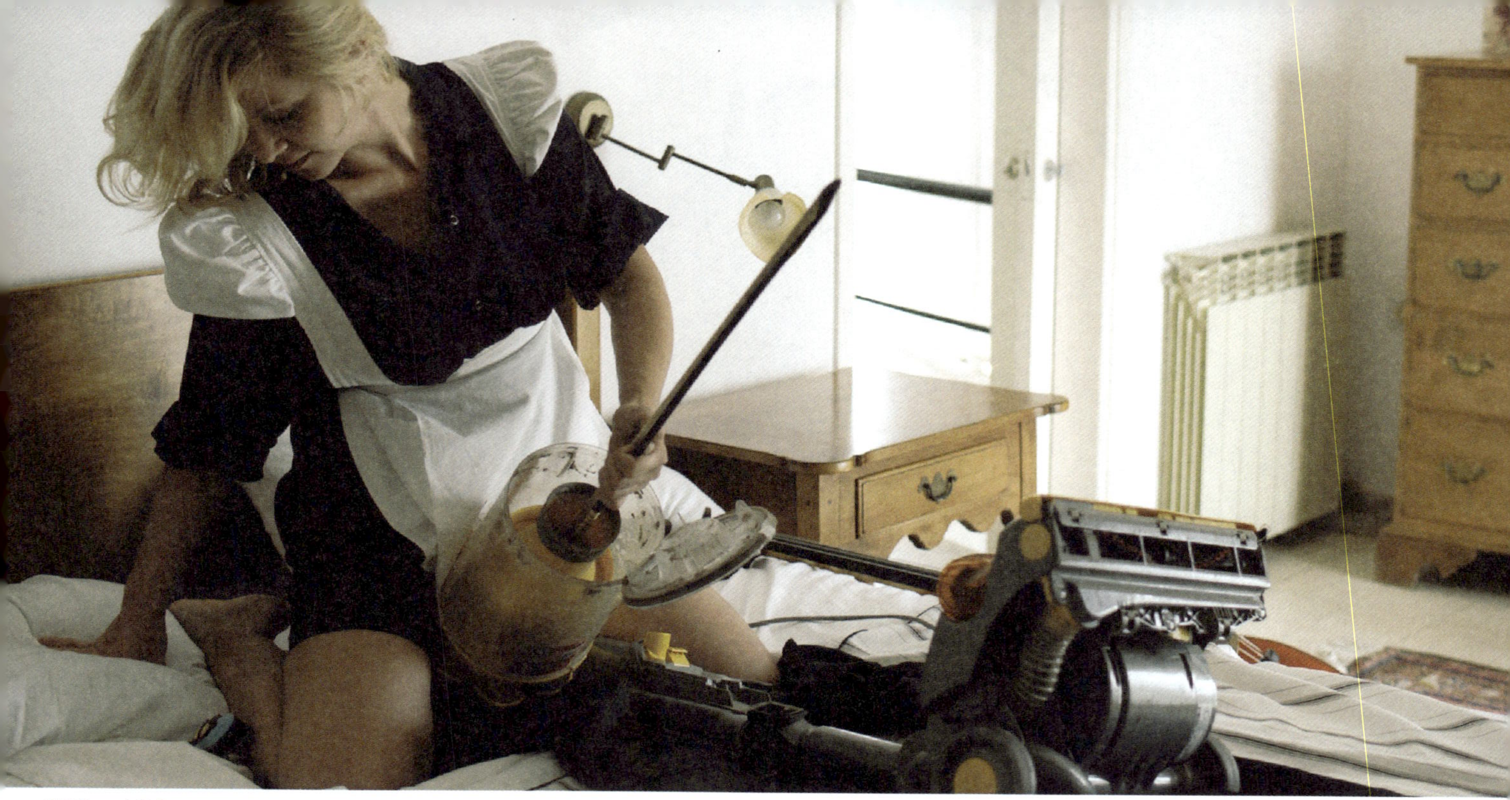

132–133

The Dust Channel, 2016. Video stills

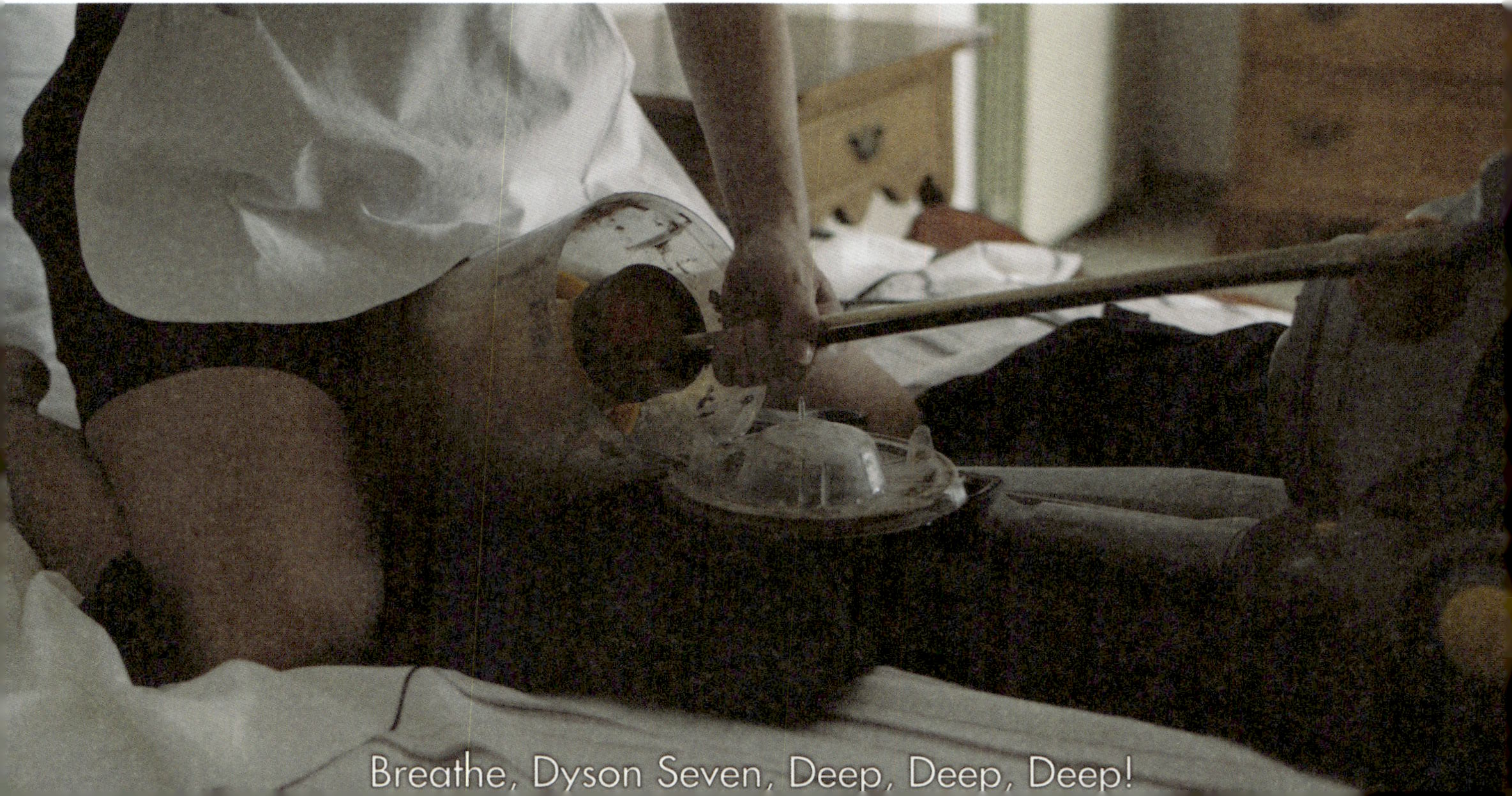
Breathe, Dyson Seven, Deep, Deep, Deep!

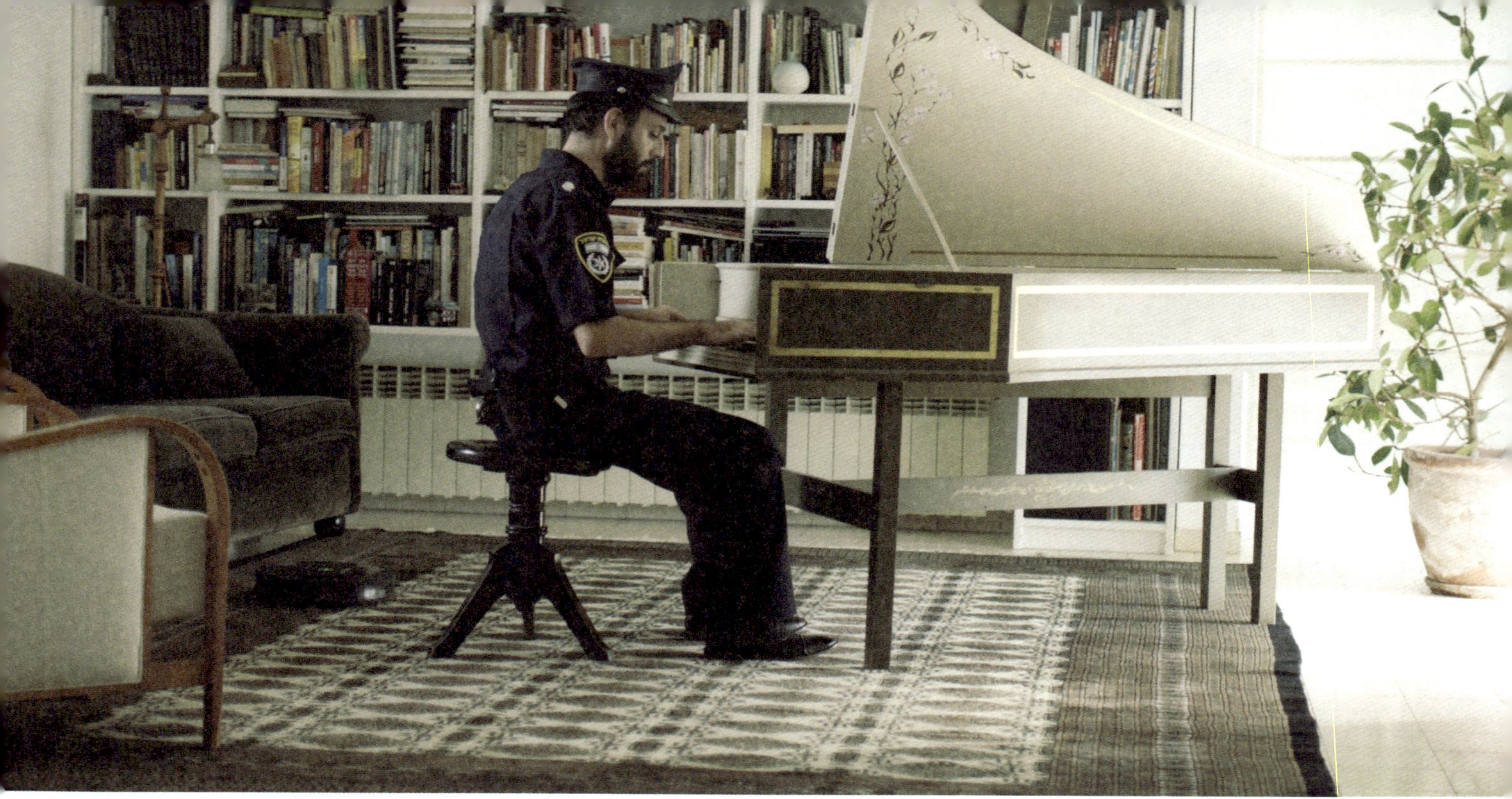

134–135 *The Dust Channel*, 2016. Video stills

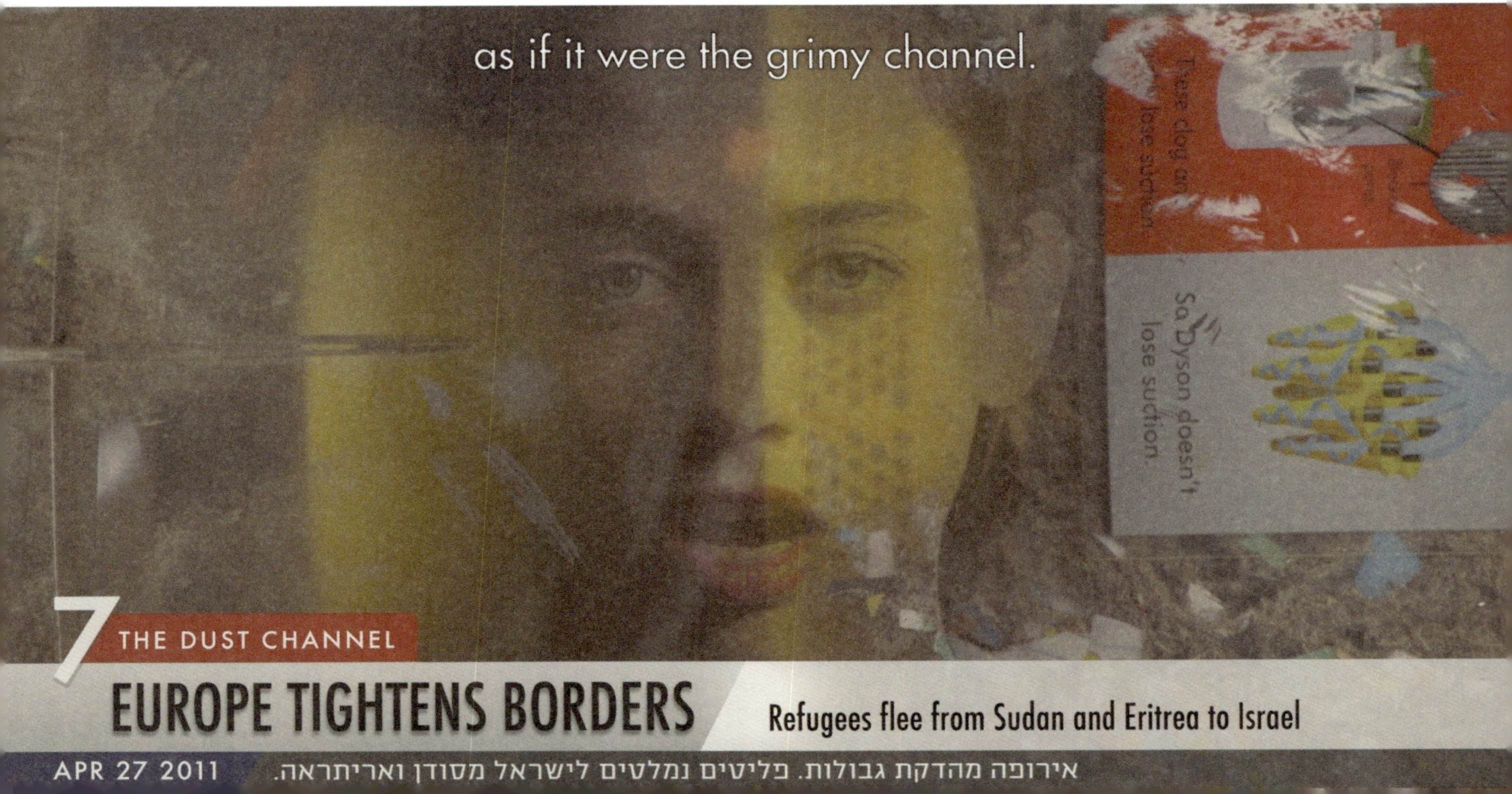
as if it were the grimy channel.
These clog an
lose suction
So Dyson doesn't
lose suction.
7 THE DUST CHANNEL
EUROPE TIGHTENS BORDERS
Refugees flee from Sudan and Eritrea to Israel
APR 27 2011
אירופה מהדקת גבולות. פליטים נמלטים לישראל מסודן ואריתראה.

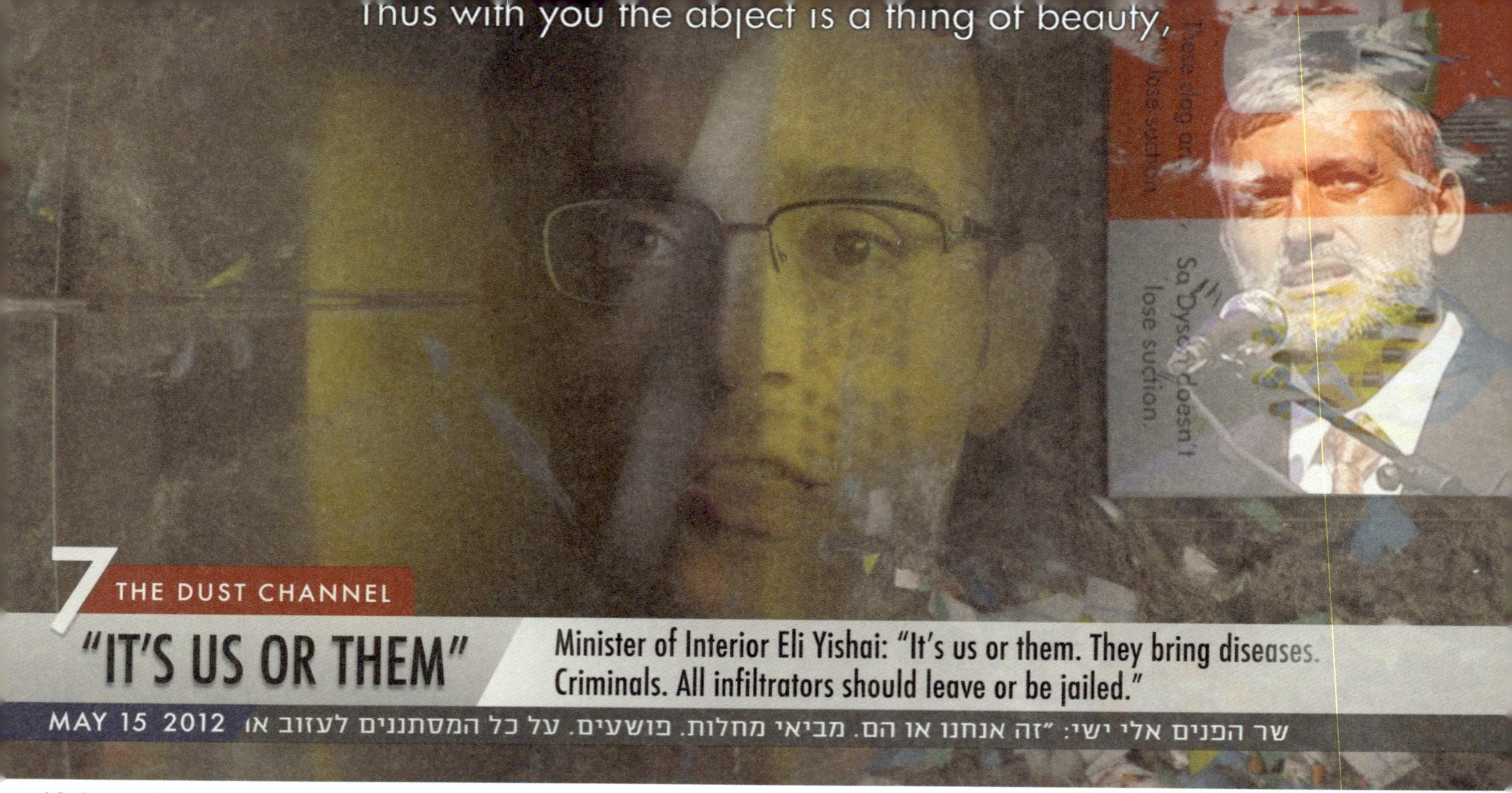

136–137

The Dust Channel, 2016. Video stills

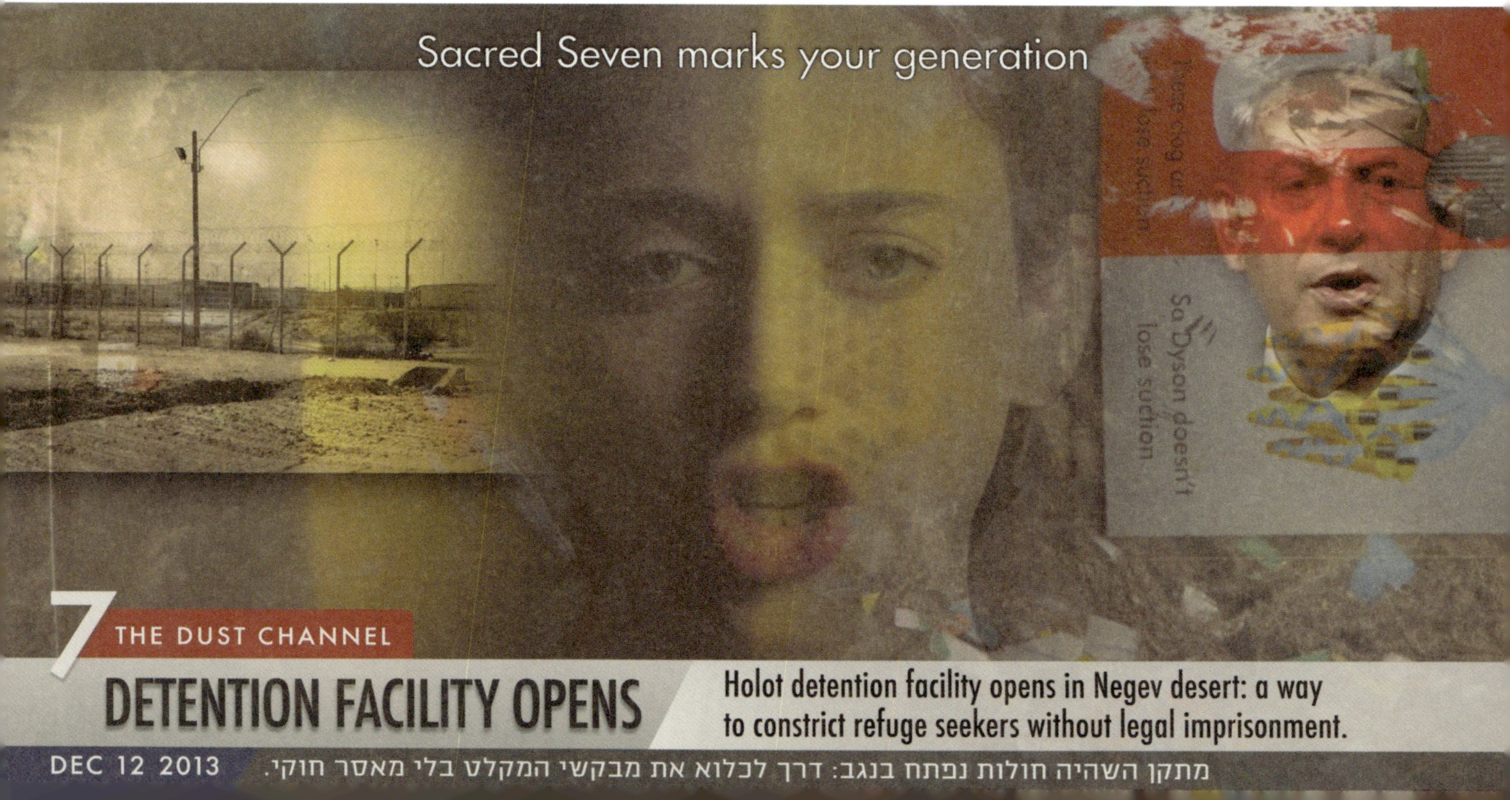

Sacred Seven marks your generation
So Dyson doesn't
lose suction
7 THE DUST CHANNEL
DETENTION FACILITY OPENS
Holot detention facility opens in Negev desert: a way
to constrict refuge seekers without legal imprisonment.
DEC 12 2013
מתקן השהיה חולות נפתח בנגב: דרך לכלוא את מבקשי המקלט בלי מאסר חוקי.

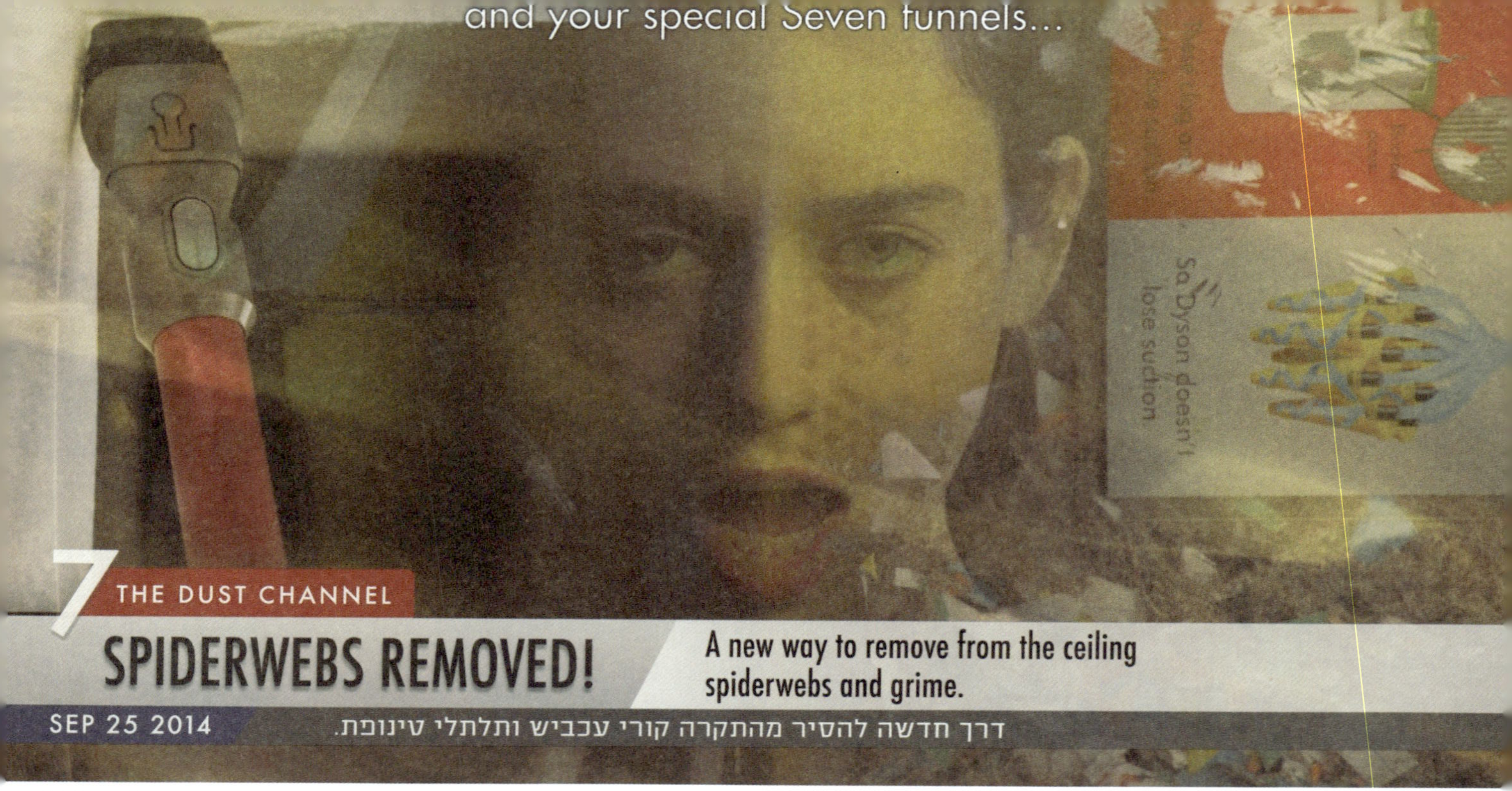

138–139

The Dust Channel, 2016. Video stills

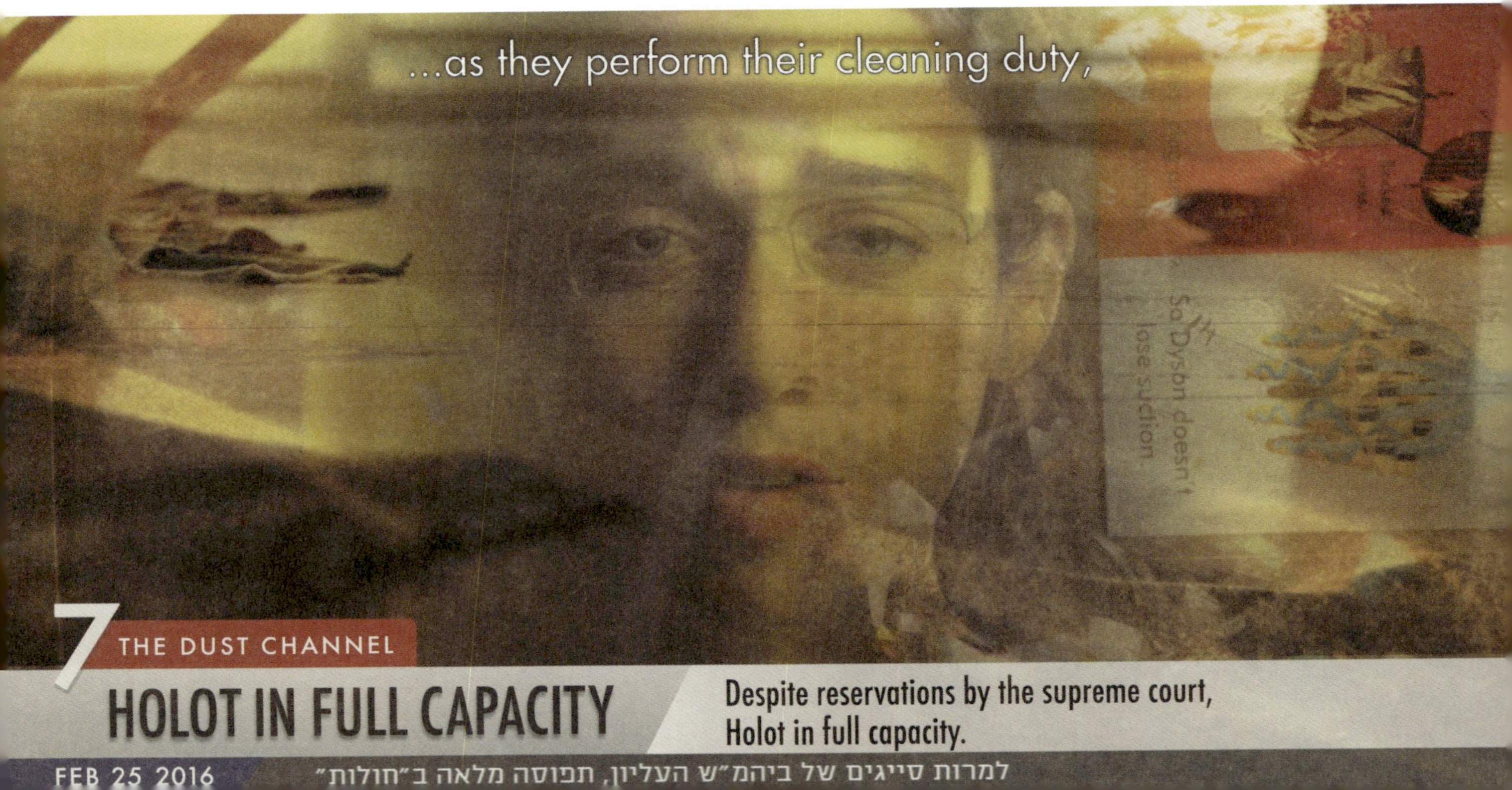

...as they perform their cleaning duty,
So Dyson doesn't lose suction.
7 THE DUST CHANNEL
HOLOT IN FULL CAPACITY
Despite reservations by the supreme court, Holot in full capacity.
FEB 25 2016
למרות סייגים של ביהמ״ש העליון, תפוסה מלאה ב״חולות״

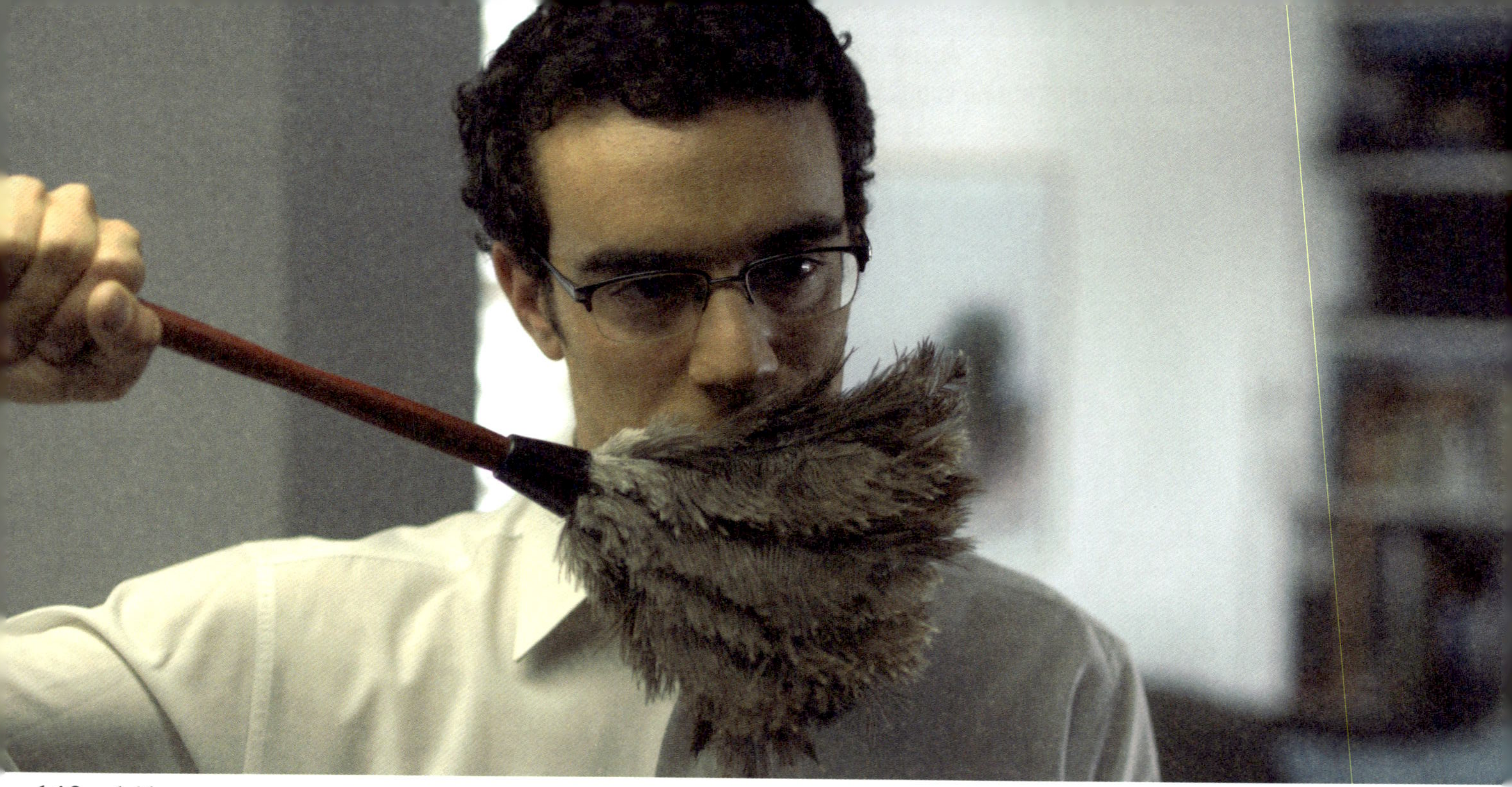

The Dust Channel, 2016. Video stills

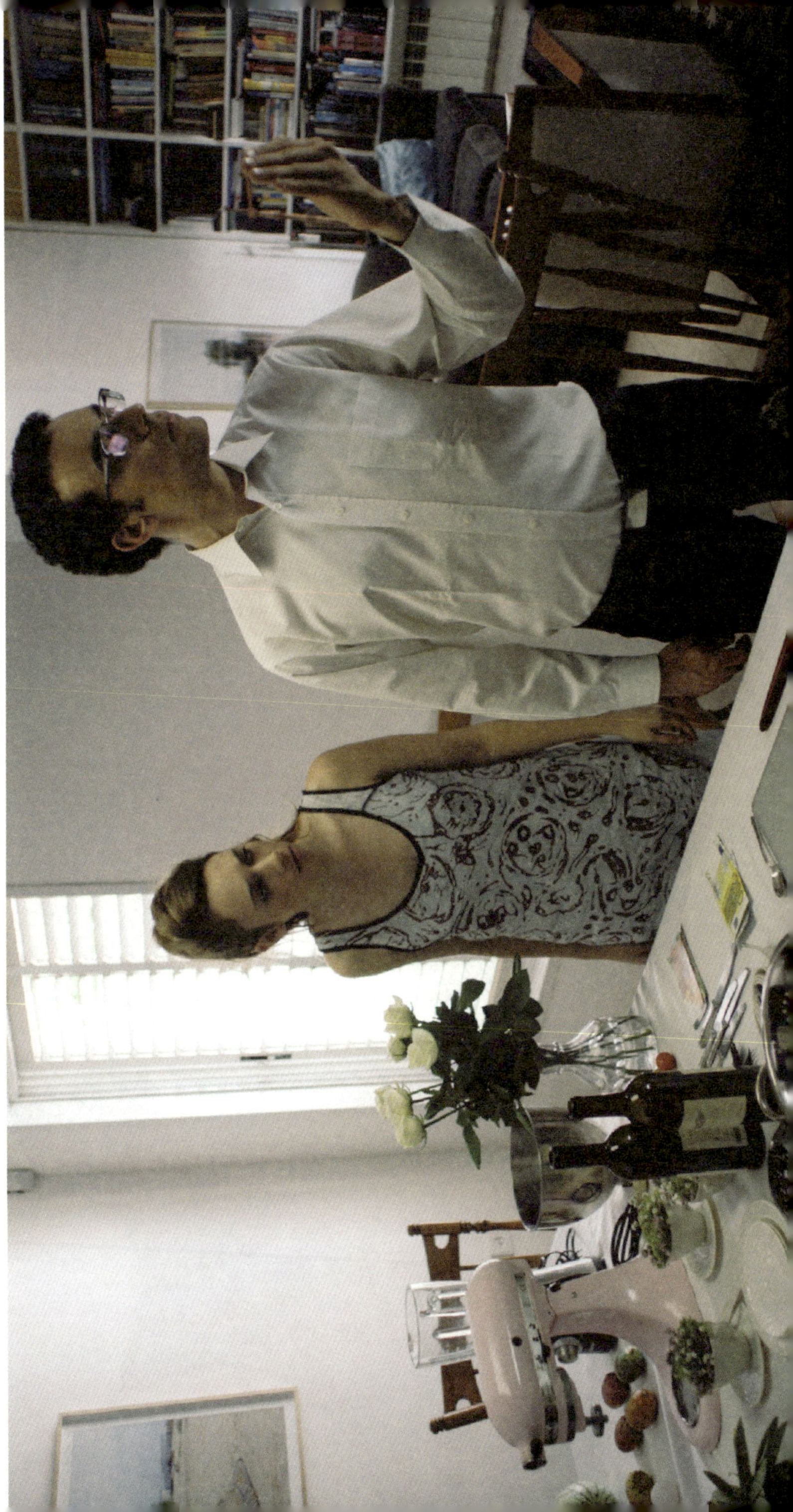

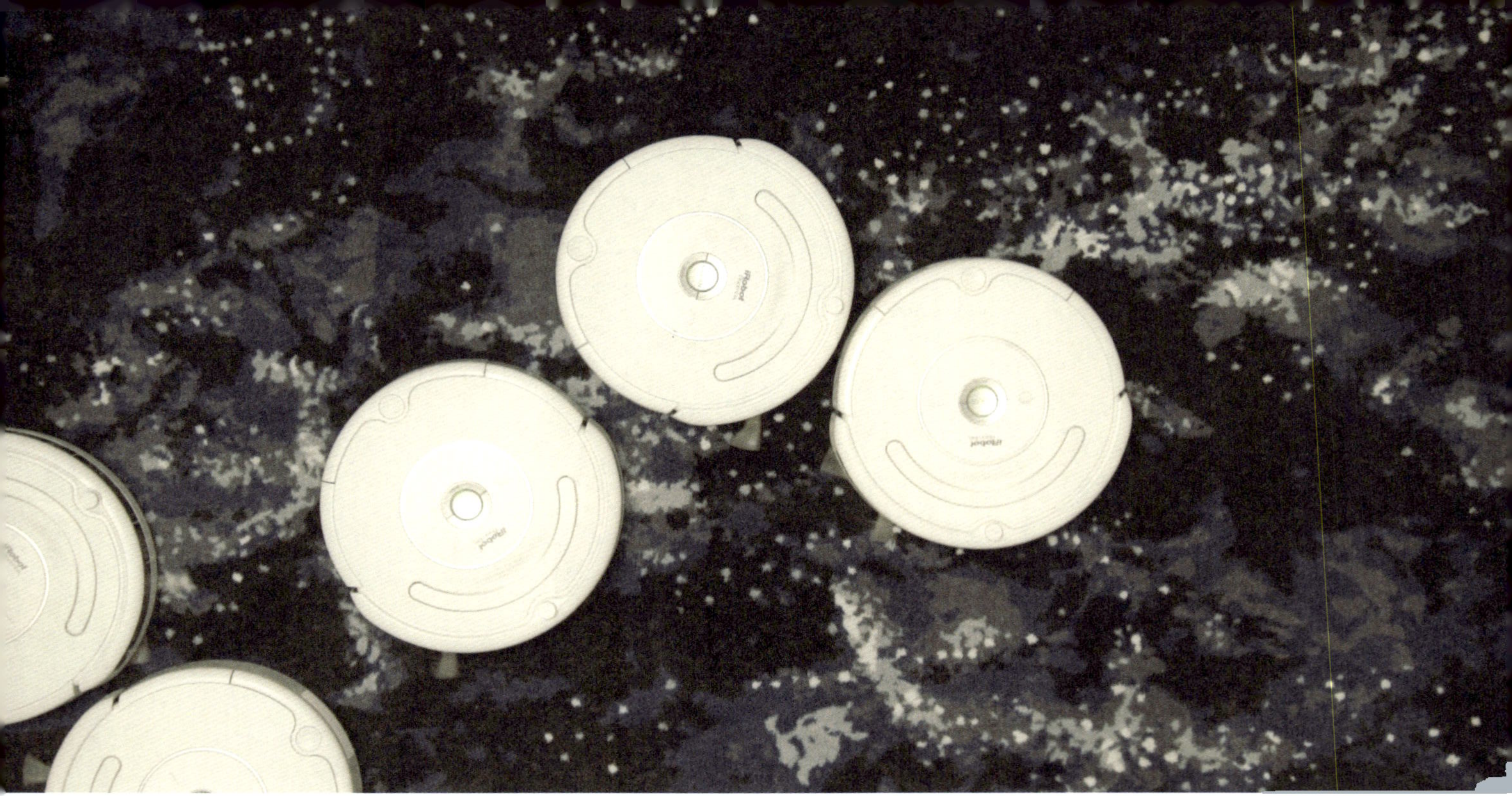

142 – 143 *The Dust Channel*, 2016. Video stills

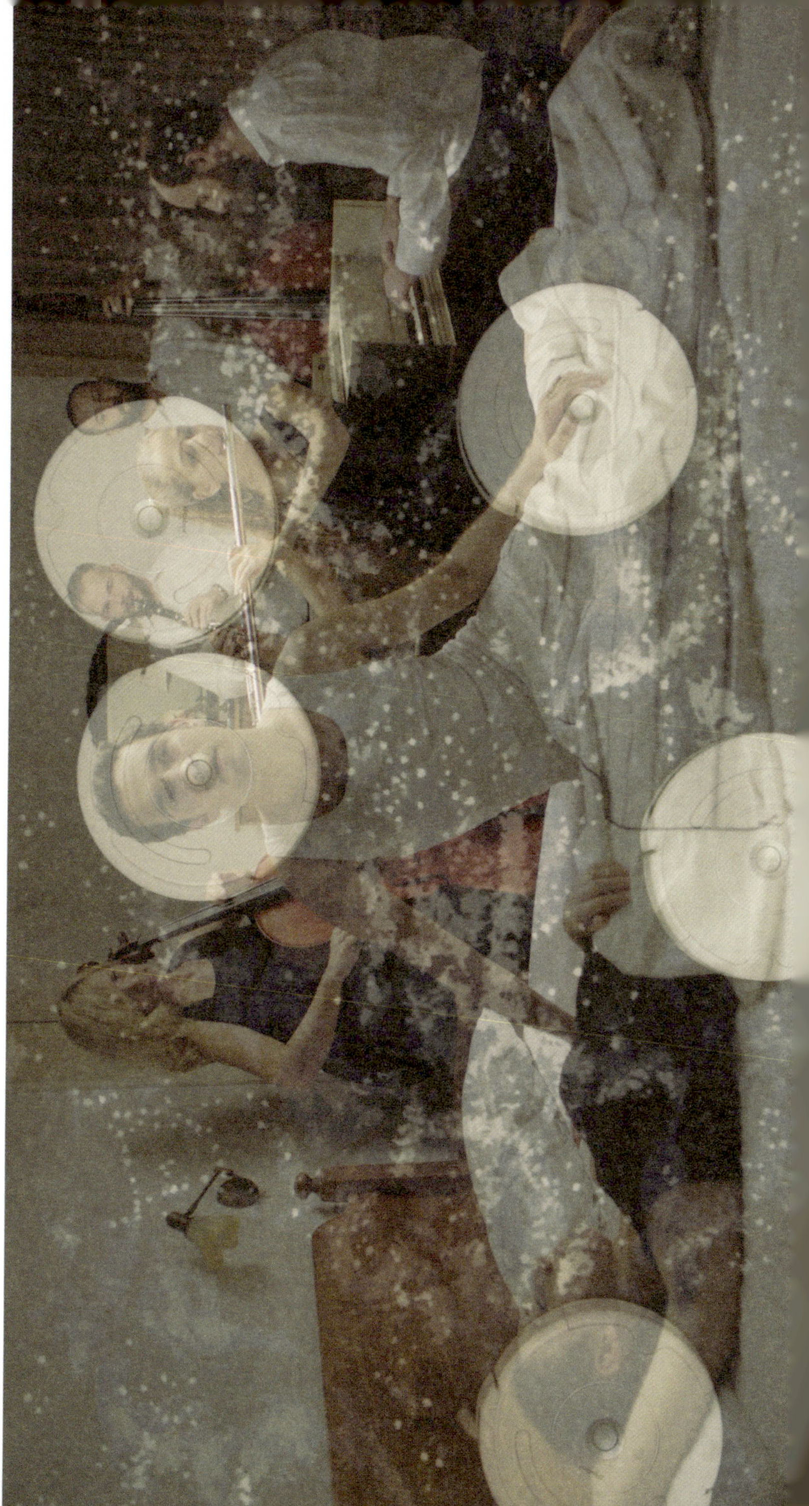

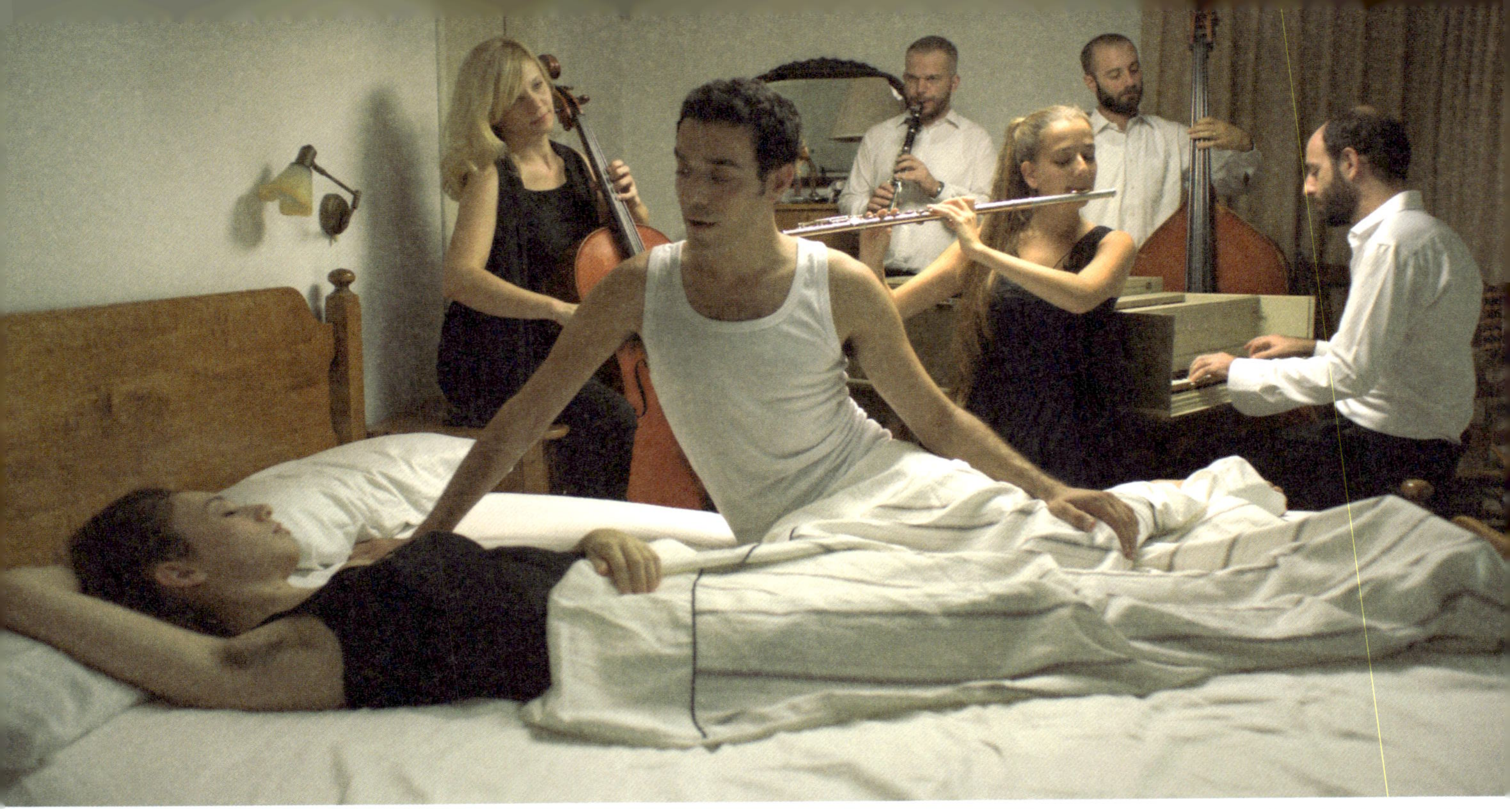

144–145 *The Dust Channel*, 2016. Video stills

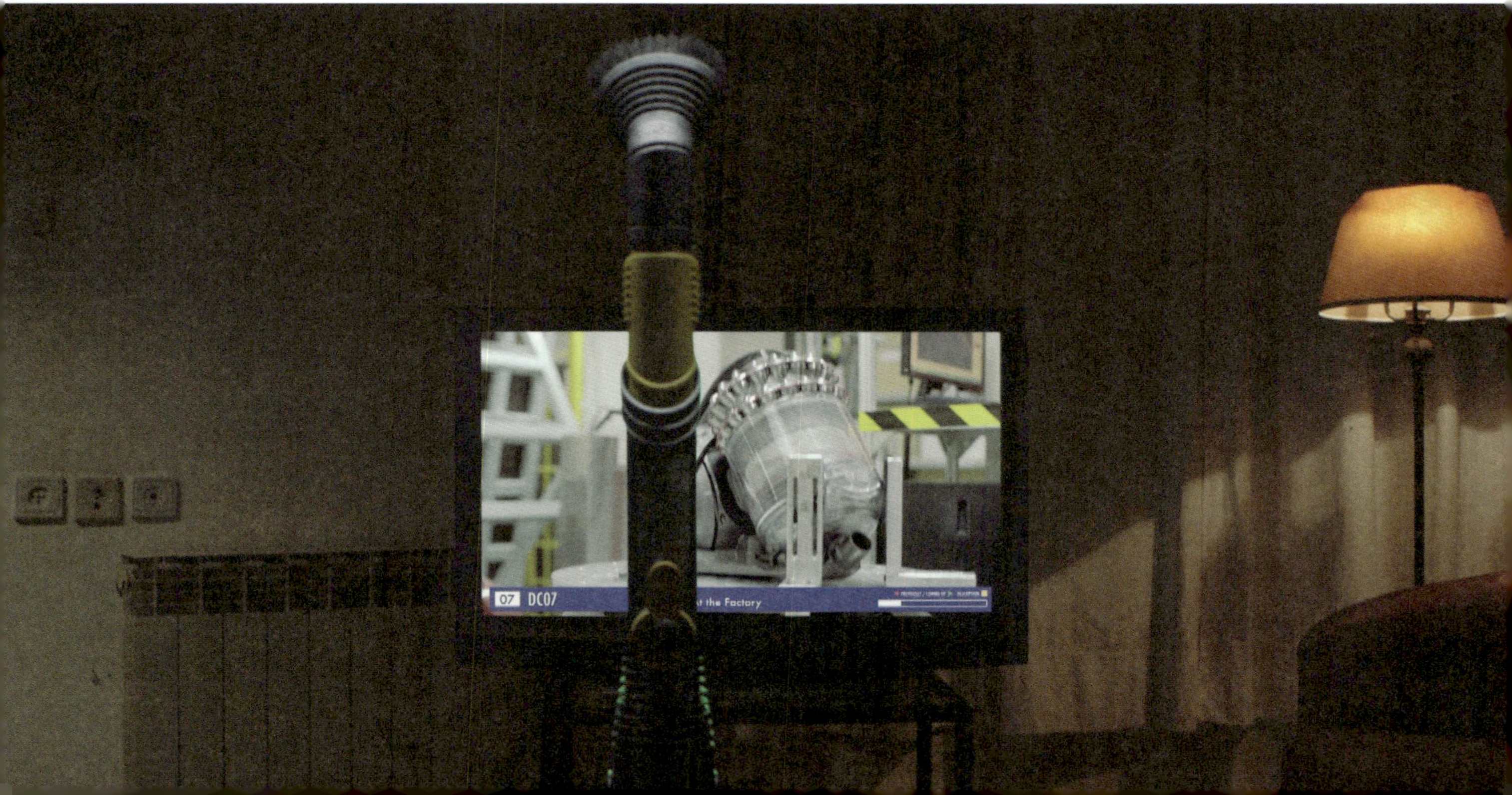
07 DC07
t the Factory

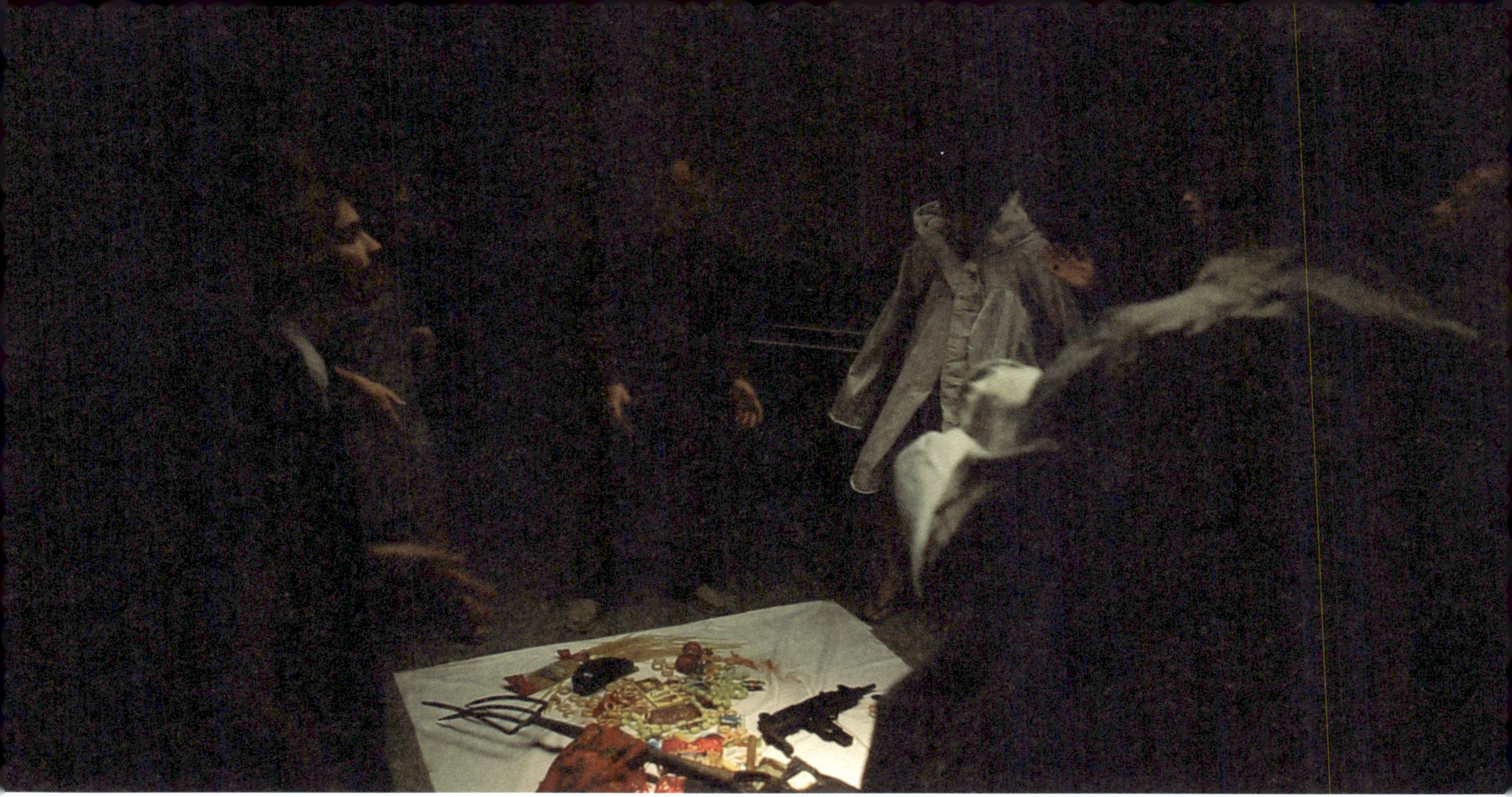

146–147

The Buried Alive Videos, 2013. Video stills

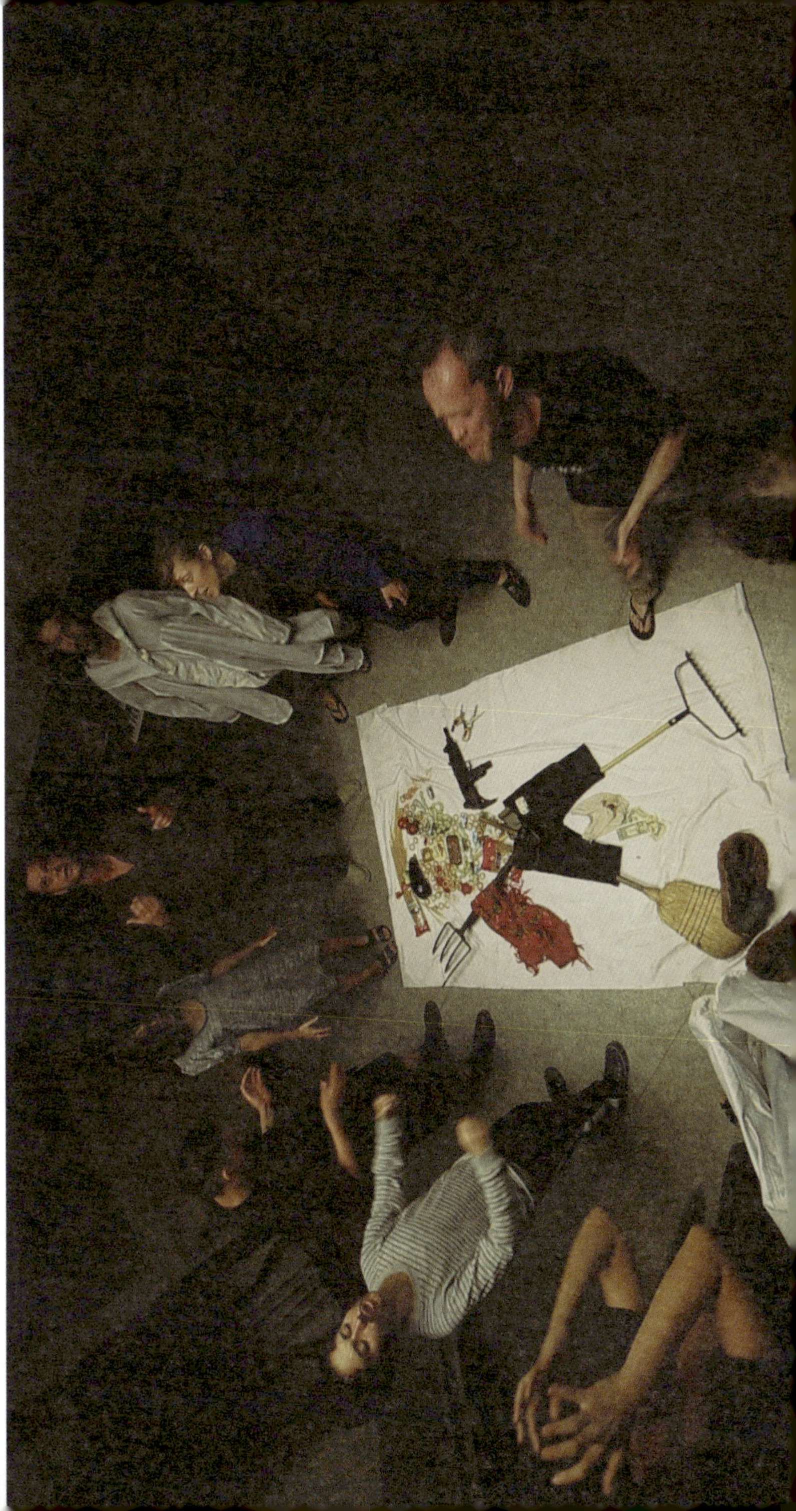

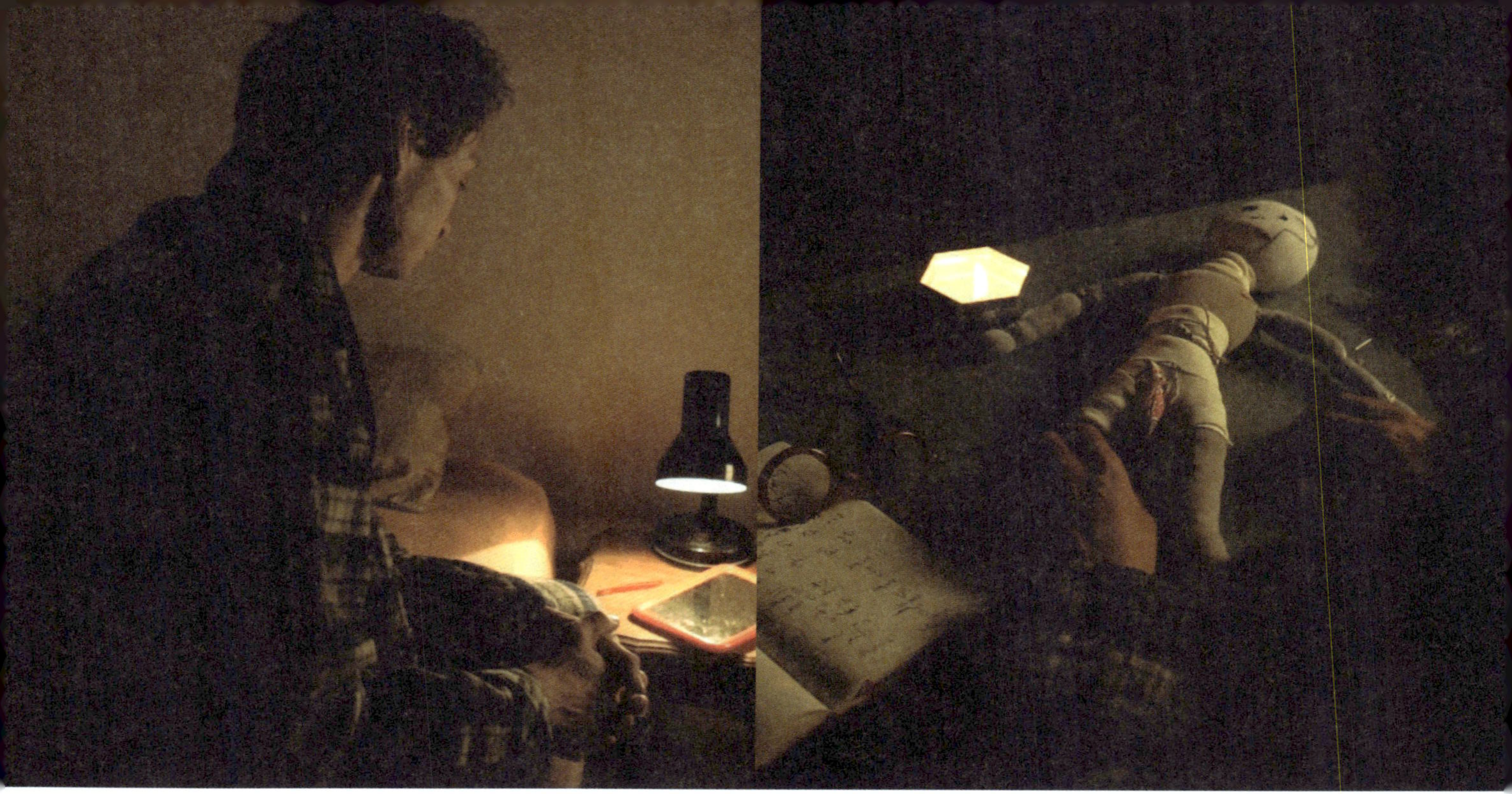

148 – 149

The Buried Alive Videos, 2013. Video stills

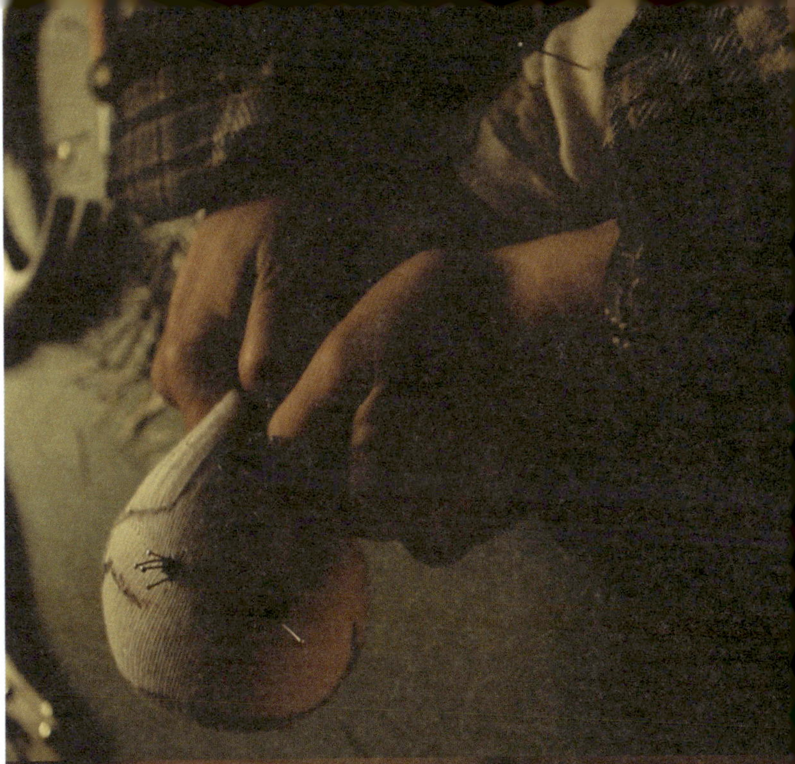
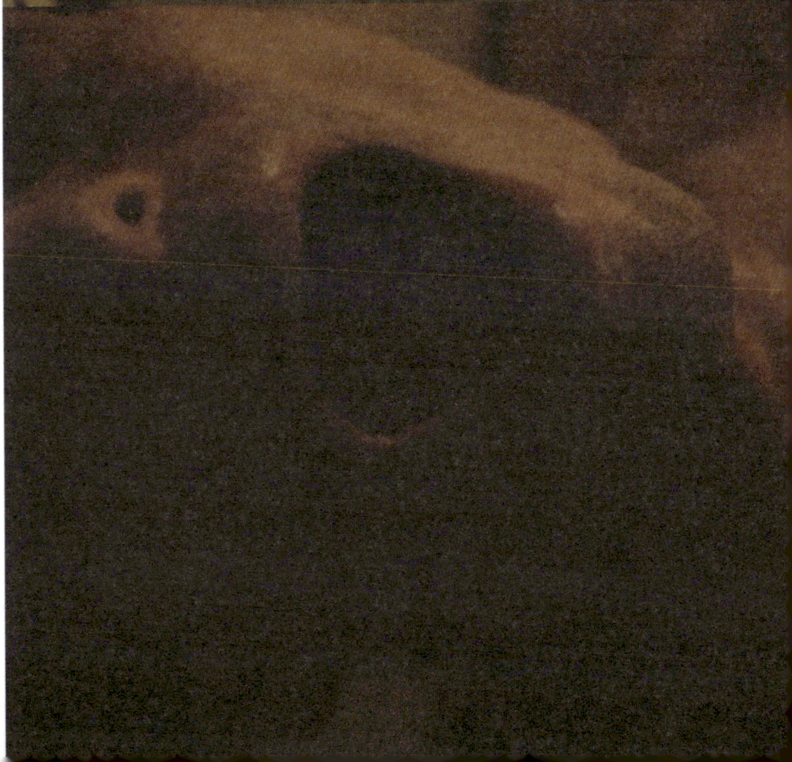

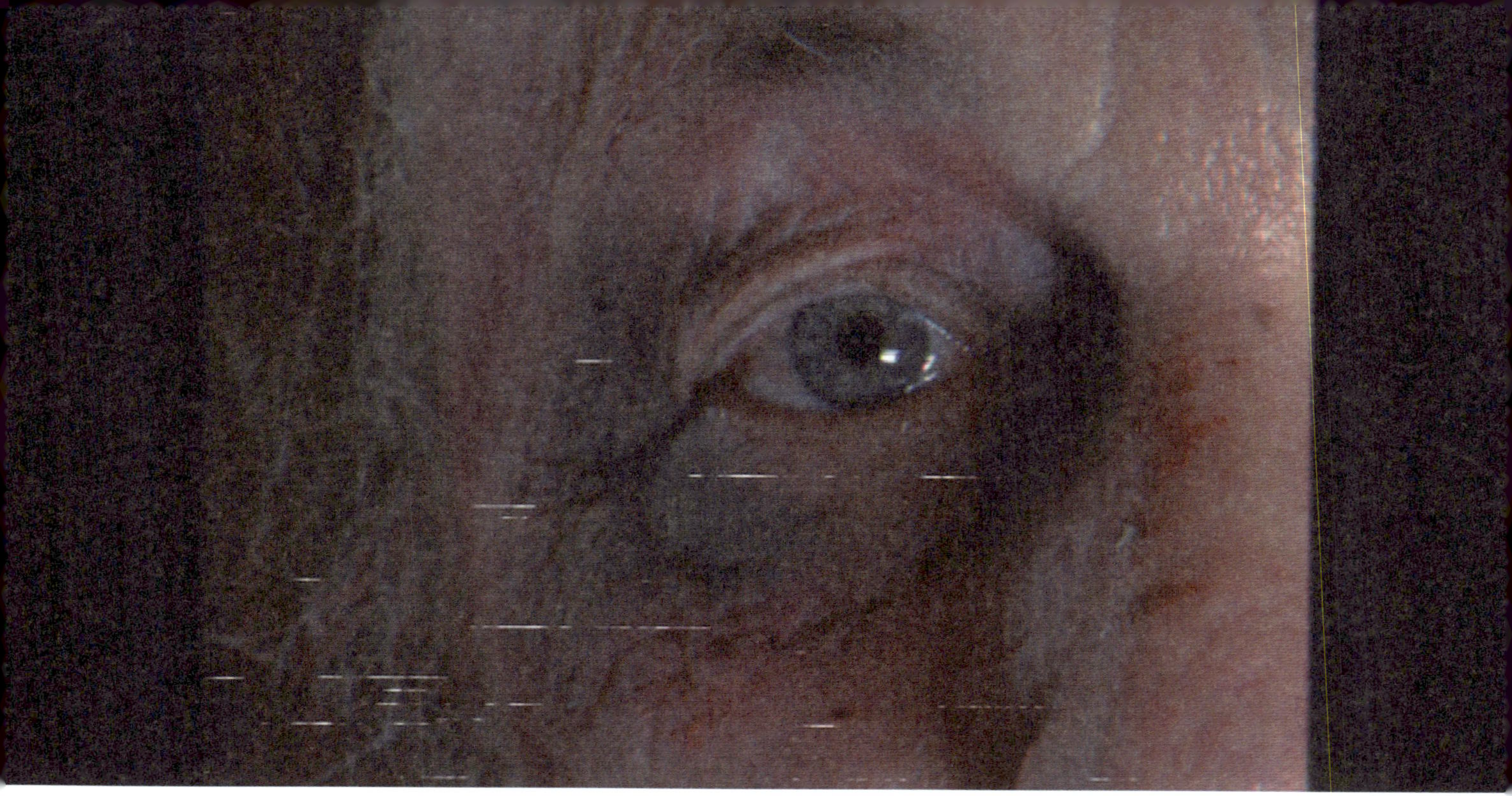

150–151

The Buried Alive Videos, 2013. Video stills

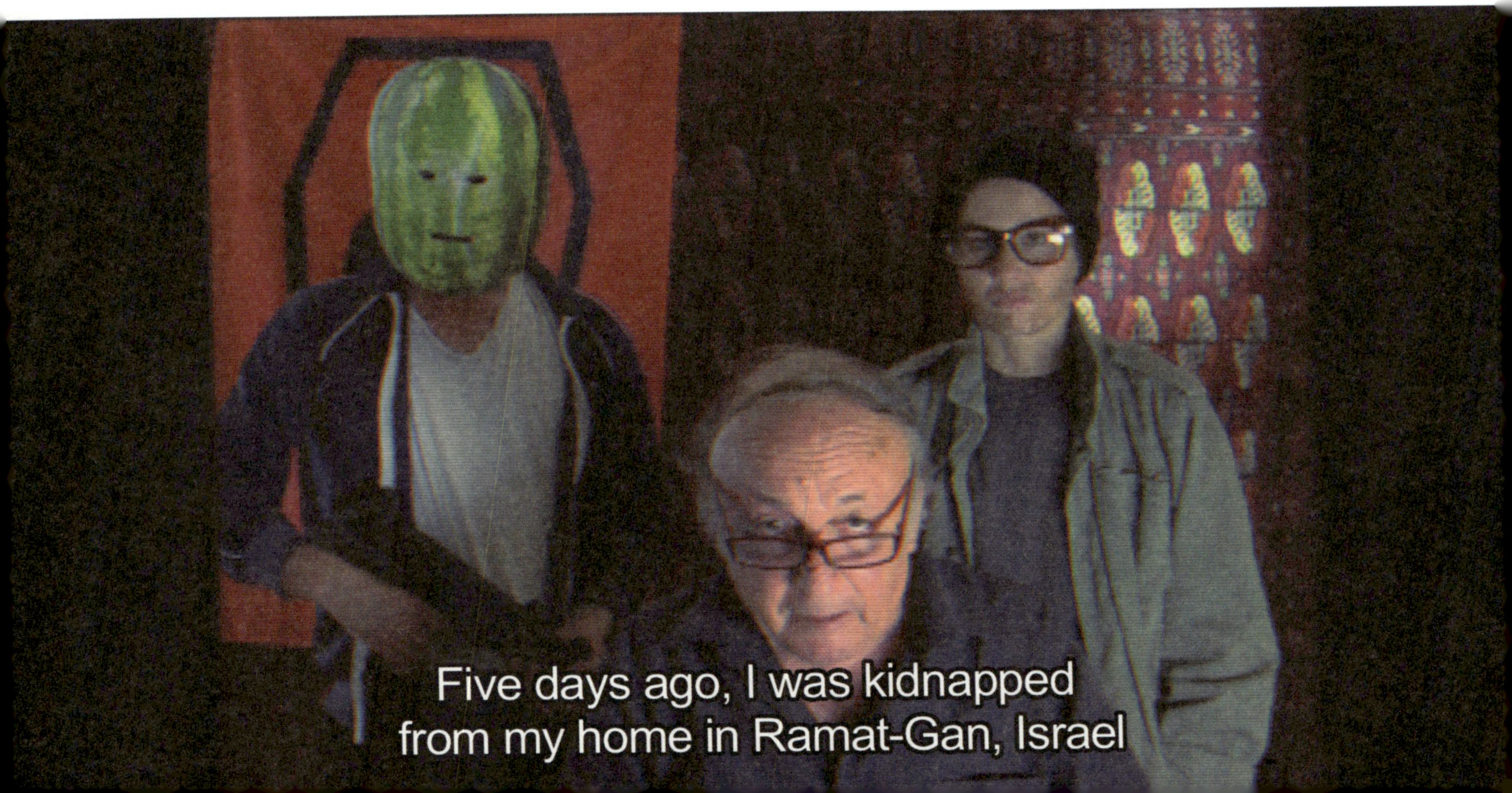
Five days ago, I was kidnapped
from my home in Ramat-Gan, Israel

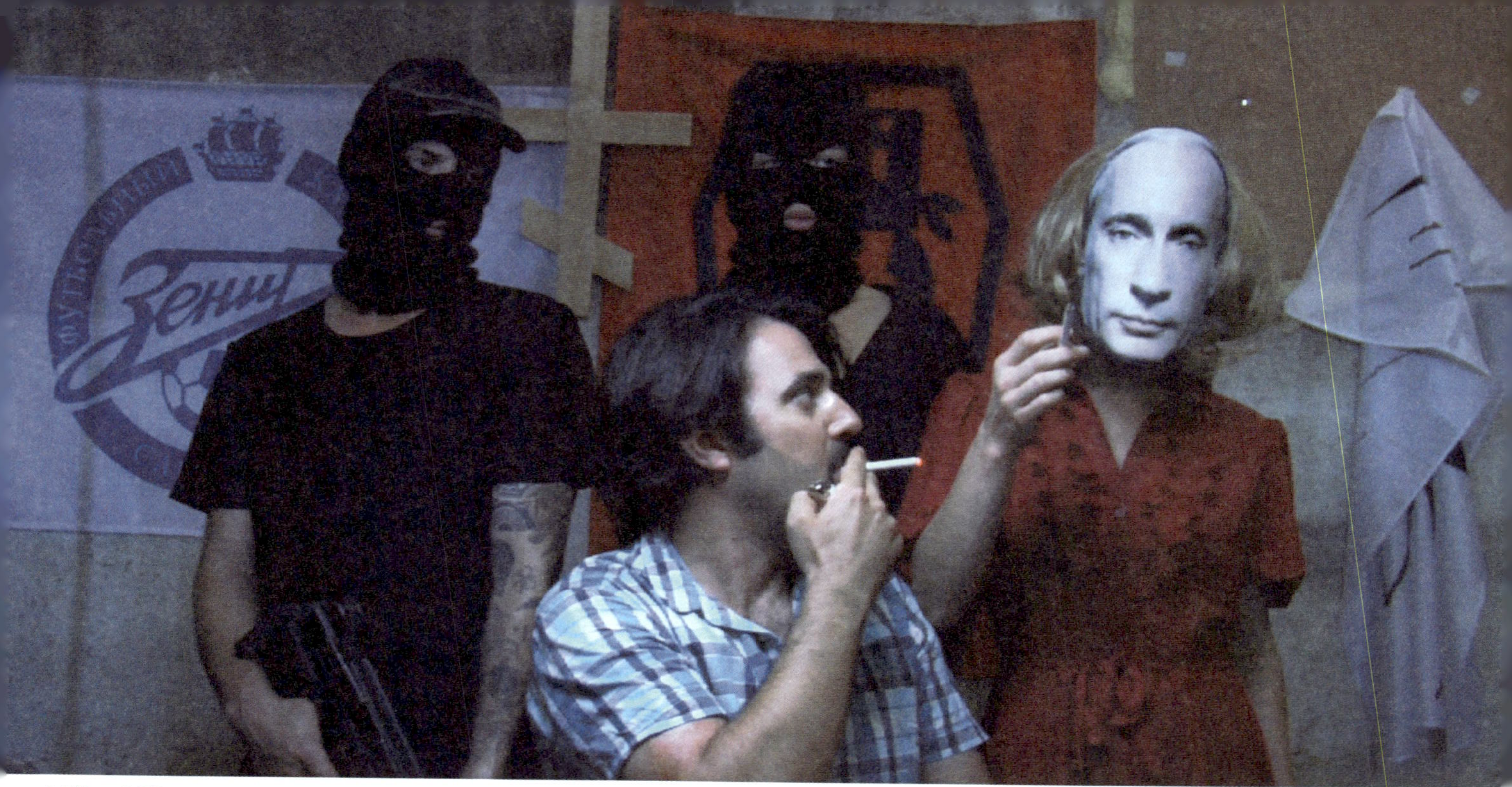

152–153

The Buried Alive Videos, 2013. Video stills

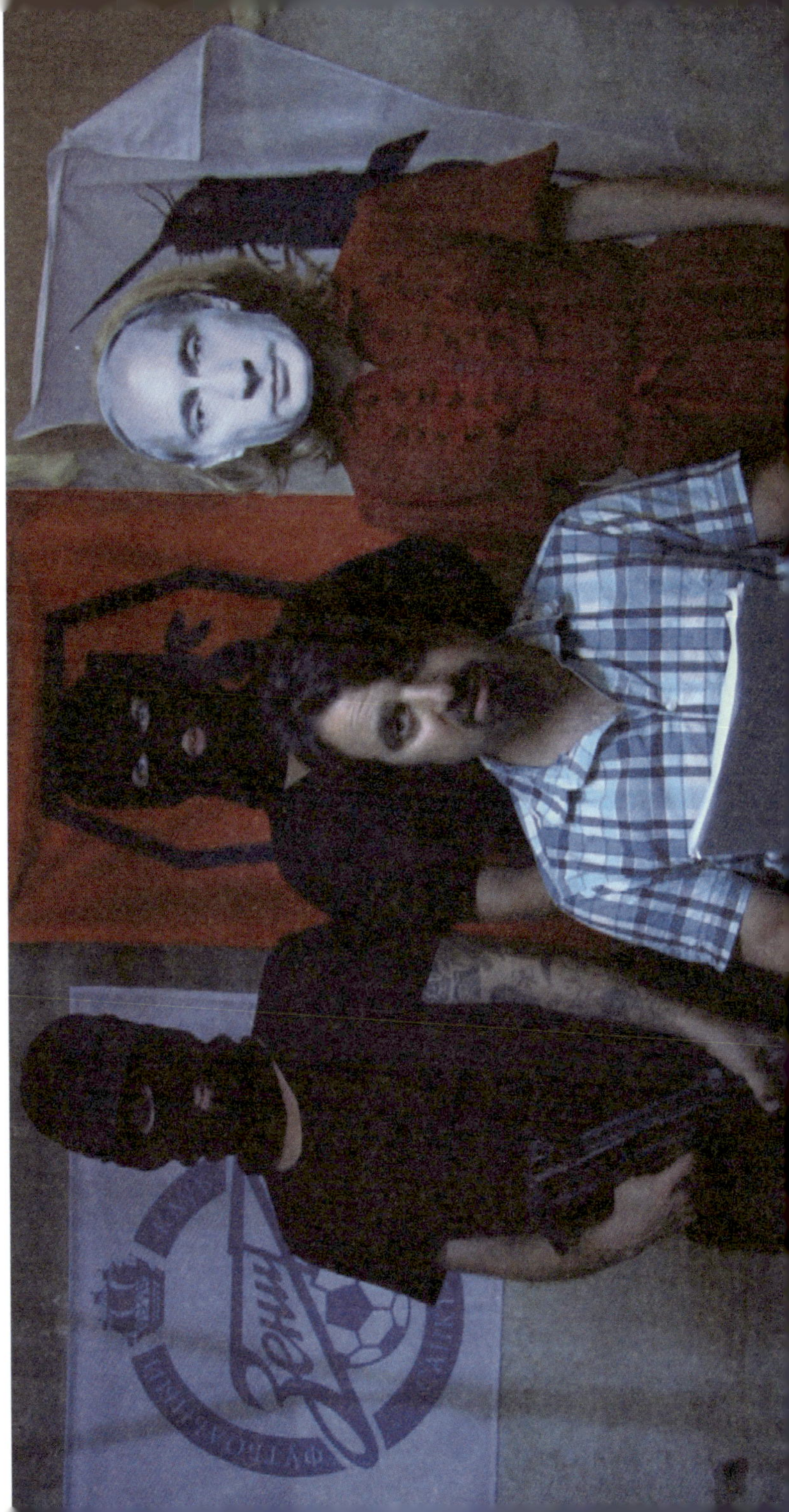

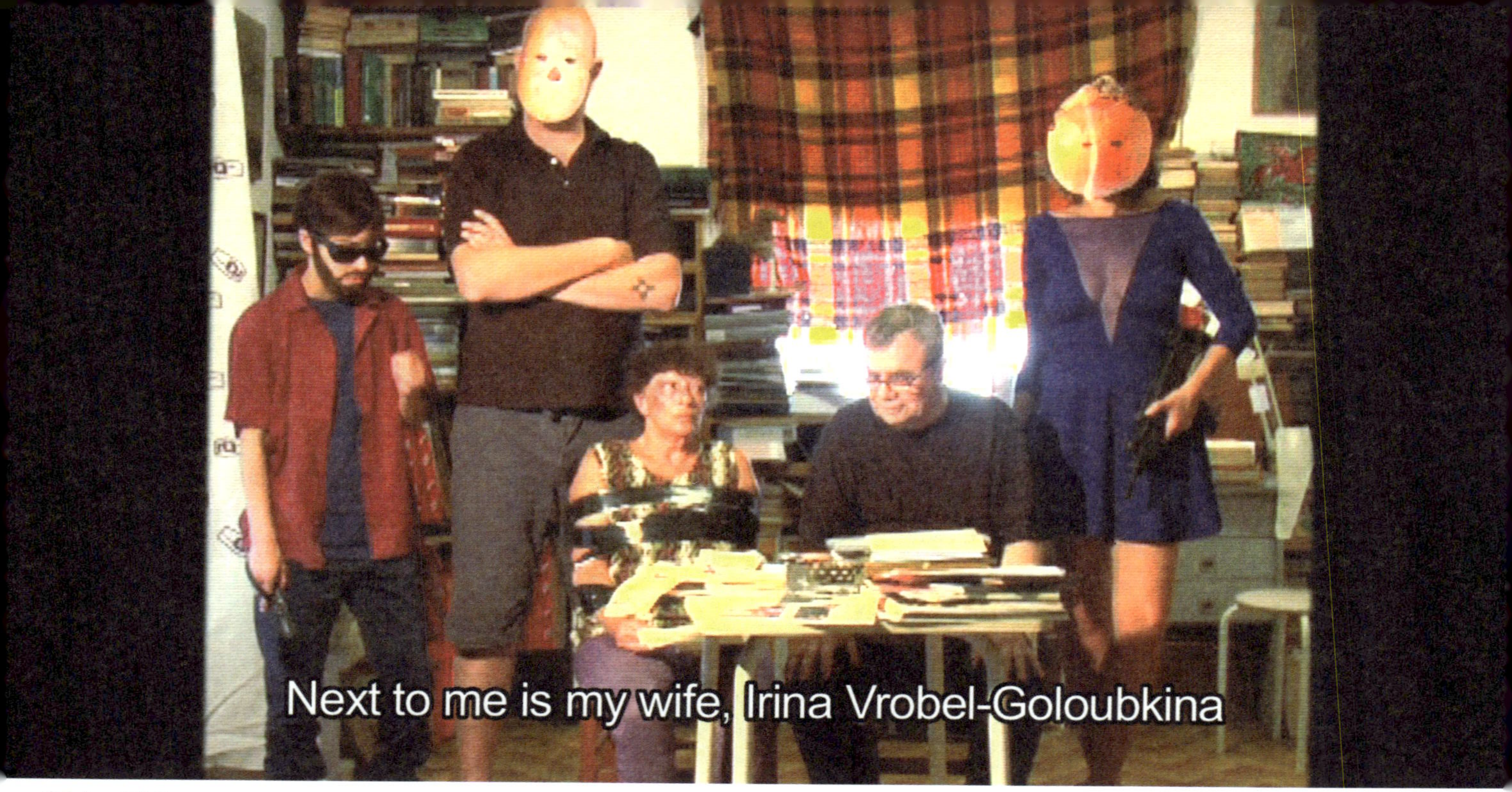

154–155 *The Buried Alive Videos*, 2013. Video stills

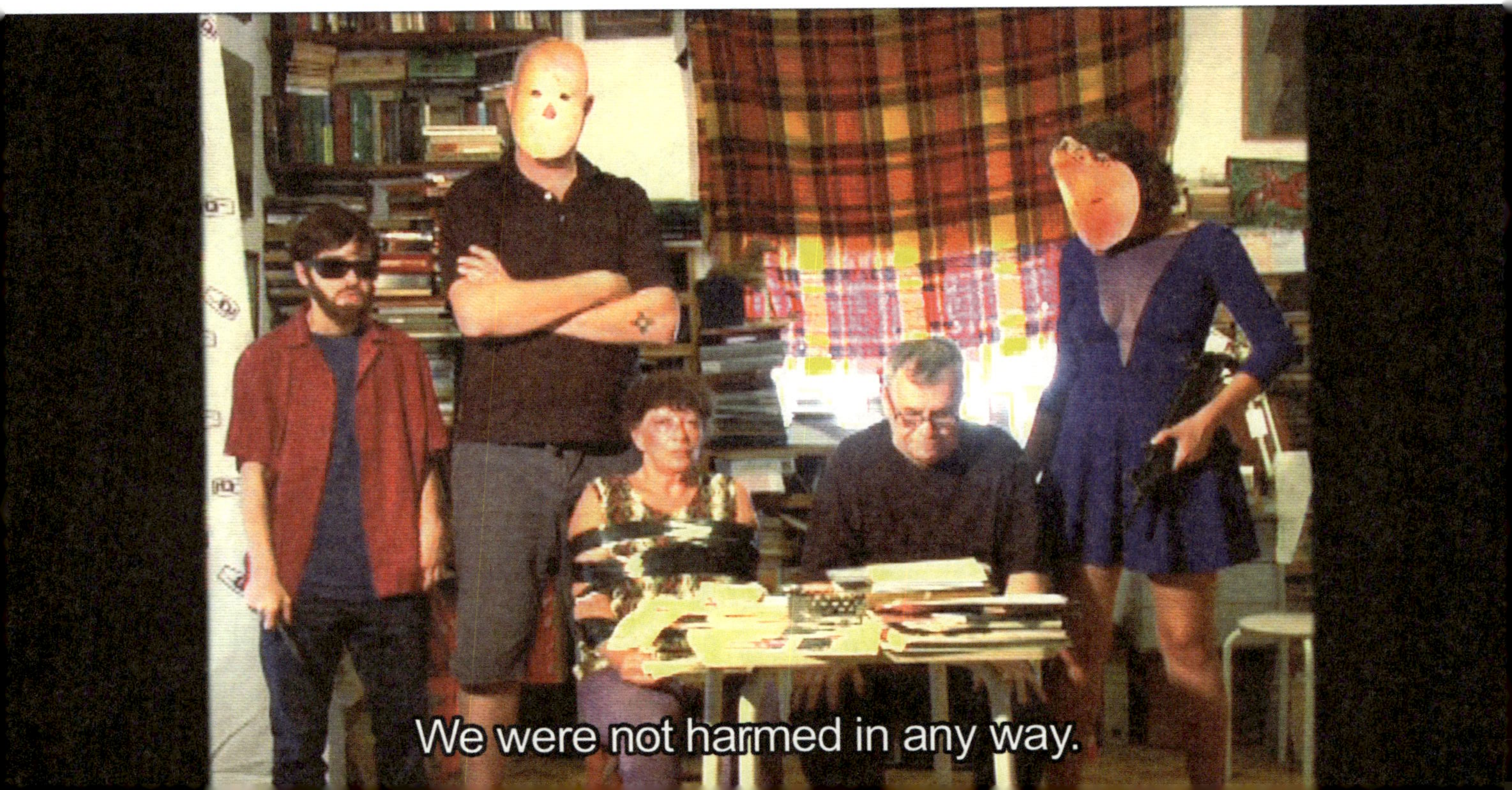
We were not harmed in any way.

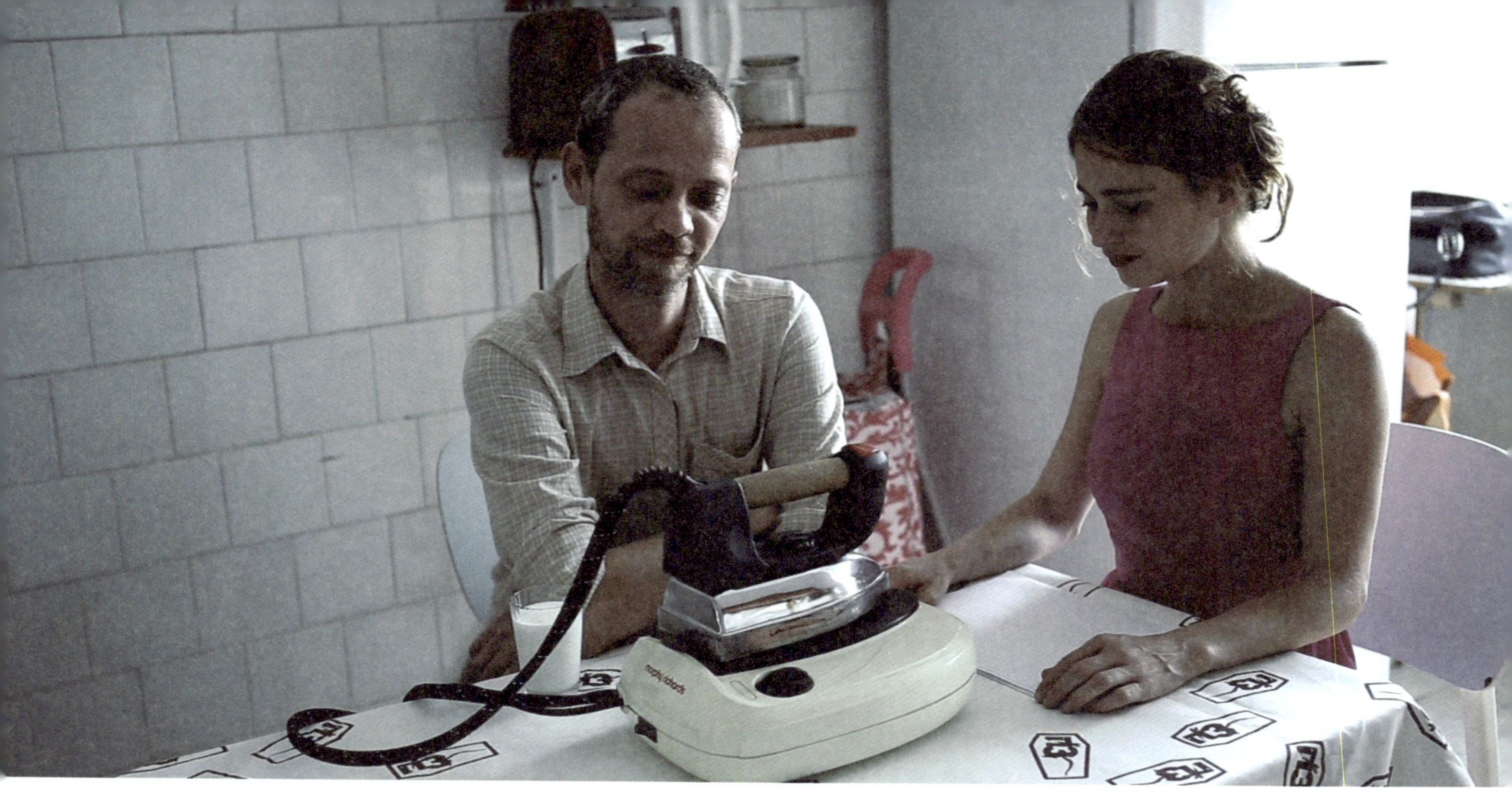

156–157 *The Buried Alive Videos*, 2013. Video stills

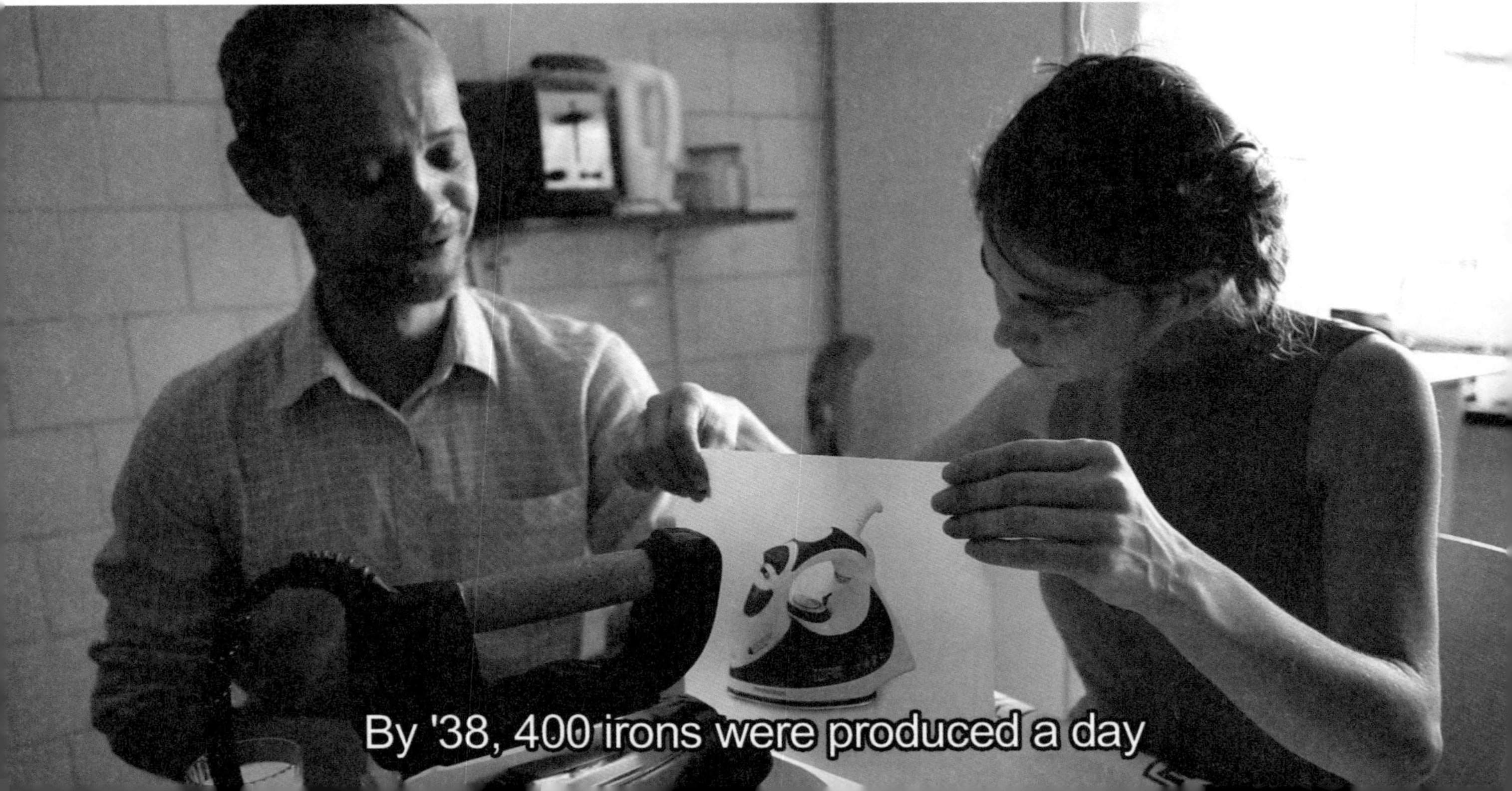
By '38, 400 irons were produced a day

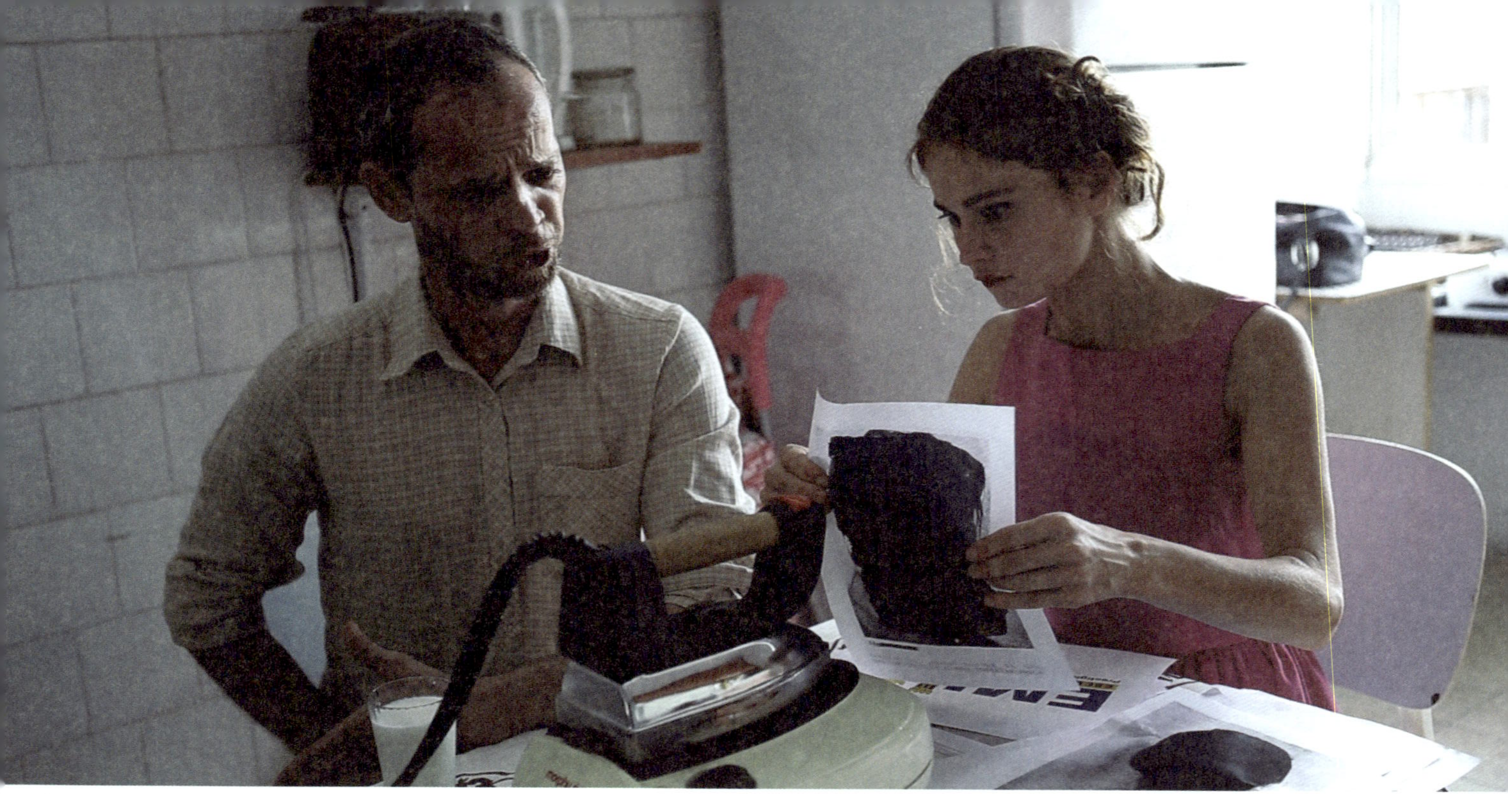

158–159 *The Buried Alive Videos*, 2013. Video stills

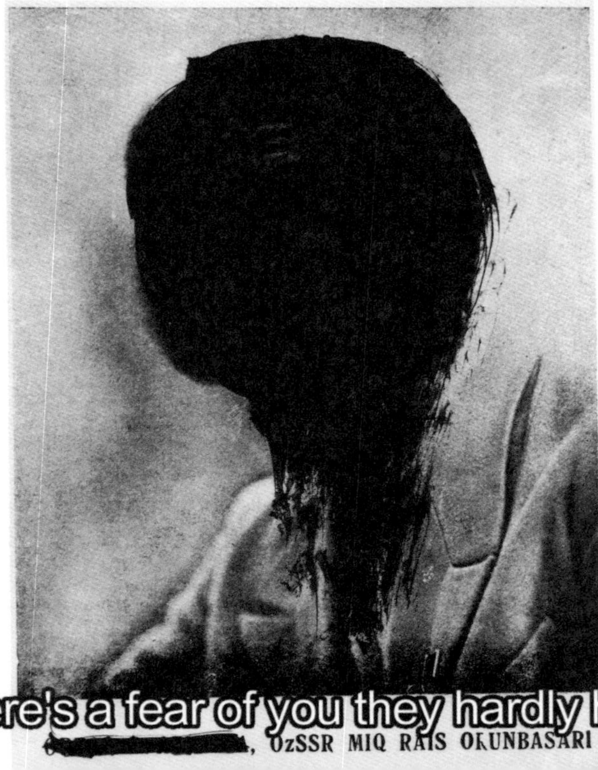
but there's a fear of you they hardly handle,
, OzSSR MIQ RAIS OKUNBASARI

Colophon

This book is published as part of the exhibition *Roee Rosen: The Mosquito-Mouse and Other Hybrids*, 31 October 2019 – 16 February 2020, Kunsthal Charlottenborg.

Publication

Editors: Anne Mikél Jensen and Roee Rosen
Design: Wrong Studio
Proofreading: James Copeland and Laura Preston
Images: Courtesy of the artist and Rosenfeld Gallery
Edition: 500
Print: Graphic Unit / Strandbygaard

Published by: Billedkunstskolernes Forlag
Kgs. Nytorv 1, 1050 København K
and Sternberg Press
Caroline Schneider
Karl-Marx-Allee 78
D-10243 Berlin
www.sternberg-press.com

Texts

Paul B. Preciado: *The Dust Files*, 2019, text commissioned for this publication.

Sergei Tret'iakov: *The Biography of the Object*, translated by Devin Fore, *October* 118, Fall 2006, pp. 57–62. © 2006 by October Magazine, Ltd. and the Massachusetts Institute of Technology.

Roee Rosen: *Vengeful Animism: On Maxim Komar-Myshkin's "Vladimir's Night"* first appeared in: Anselm Franke (editor), *Animism: Modernity Through the Looking Glass*, Vienna, Generali Foundation, 2011, pp. 104–107.

The Buried Alive Manifesto first appeared in: Ekaterina Degot and David Riff (editors), *Monday Begins on Saturday, Bergen Assembly 2013*, Berlin, Sternberg Press, 2013, pp. 188–189.

The following texts are excerpted from Roee Rosen: *Maxim Komar-Myshkin, Vladimir's Night*, Berlin, Sternberg Press, 2014:

Animation Chants for Commodities: DC07 Vacuum Cleaner, p. 117.
Animation Chants for Commodities: A Little Iron, p. 115.
Animation Chants for Commodities: A Hybrid, p. 131.
A Complete History of Russia in Jokes (Incomplete), pp. 165–169.

Exhibition

Artist: Roee Rosen
Curator and producer: Anne Mikél Jensen
Communication: Jeannie Møller Haltrup
Technical team: Keith Allen, Desmond Church, Brian Ravnholt Jepsen, Chris McSherry and Nikolaj Phillipsen.

Kunsthal Charlottenborg

Director: Michael Thouber
Curator: Henriette Bretton-Meyer
Producer and cinema programmer: Anne Mikél Jensen
Exhibition coordinator: Gry Stangegård Schneider
Technical Coordinator: Brian Ravnholt Jepsen
Head of Visitor Services: Henrik Kræmmer
Event Coordinator: Michelle Korbø Moran
Communications Manager: Jeannie Møller Haltrup
Assistants: Emilie Victoria Stoffer Arnold, Marie Amalie Skinnebach and Sarah Pihl Petersen
Art hosts: Azita Tadayoni, Benedikte Munk Randløv, Frida Greve, Ida Raselli, Jonathan Carl, Madeleine Andersson, Maria Heitmann, Pernille Vincents, Steffen Kvåle, Tilda Lundbohm.

The exhibition and the publication are supported by the Grosserer L. F. Foght Foundation, the Knud Højgaard Foundation, the Obel Family Foundation and the Danish Arts Foundation.

ISBN 978-91-863243-88-3 (Billedkunstskolernes Forlag)

ISBN 978-3-95679-545-9 (Sternberg Press)

Distributed by The MIT Press, Art Data, and Les presses du réel